Praise for

Chart Patterns

by Bruce M. Kamich, CMT

"In these days of computer-aided technical analysis, we often forget the basics. Worse yet, many plunge in without ever learning them, only to wonder later why they are having trouble. Complexity and speed are now the name of the game, but underlying modern technical analysis there are a few valuable patterns that have stood the test of time, patterns that depict the basic market mechanism at work. For those who want to understand what is going on and who want to hear the message of the markets, Mr. Kamich's exposition of these core TA patterns will prove invaluable."

 —JOHN BOLLINGER, CFA, CMT
  www.BollingerBands.com

"Price is a fact. And price leaves patterns. This wonderful book, written by Bruce Kamich, will give the reader insights into what investors are really doing by identifying and following their buying and selling patterns. Learn about the pioneers who identified these patterns and where they typically form during a stock's normal life-cycle."

 —RALPH J. ACAMPORA, CMT
  Director, Altaira Wealth Management S.A.

"Kamich's *Chart Patterns* is the perfect resource for those not yet using candlesticks and for those who are. Whether you use Nison candlesticks or bar charts, the tactics and strategies you use in the market should be clear, and Kamich does a great job of detailing them. While candlesticks (if properly used) excel at giving reversals, they do not give price targets. And using price patterns is a prime way we determine targets for our clients."

 —STEVE NISON, CMT
  President, Candlestick.com and author of *Japanese Candlestick Charting Techniques*
  www.candlecharts.com

"*Chart Patterns* takes us through the thought process an analyst or trader should use. Kamich looks at myriad patterns, illustrating how they work, when they work, how to use them, and what to do when they don't work. Any serious student of trading and investing will benefit from this methodical study of chart patterns."

    —PHILIP J. ROTH, CMT

        Chief Technical Market Analyst, Miller Tabak & Co, LLC

CHART
PATTERNS

Related titles also available from BLOOMBERG PRESS

Bloomberg MARKET ESSENTIALS

TECHNICAL ANALYSIS

CHART
PATTERNS

Bruce M.
KAMICH, CMT

BLOOMBERG PRESS

NEW YORK

BLOOMBERG, BLOOMBERG ANYWHERE, BLOOMBERG.COM, BLOOMBERG MARKET ESSENTIALS, *Bloomberg Markets*, BLOOMBERG NEWS, BLOOMBERG PRESS, BLOOMBERG PROFESSIONAL, BLOOMBERG RADIO, BLOOMBERG TELEVISION, and BLOOMBERG TRADEBOOK are trademarks and service marks of Bloomberg Finance L.P. ("BFLP"), a Delaware limited partnership, or its subsidiaries. The BLOOMBERG PROFESSIONAL service (the "BPS") is owned and distributed locally by BFLP and its subsidiaries in all jurisdictions other than Argentina, Bermuda, China, India, Japan, and Korea (the "BLP Countries"). BFLP is a wholly-owned subsidiary of Bloomberg L.P. ("BLP"). BLP provides BFLP with all global marketing and operational support and service for these products and distributes the BPS either directly or through a non–BFLP subsidiary in the BLP Countries. All rights reserved.

This publication contains the author's opinions and is designed to provide accurate and authoritative information. It is sold with the understanding that the author, publisher, and Bloomberg L.P. are not engaged in rendering legal, accounting, investment-planning, or other professional advice. The reader should seek the services of a qualified professional for such advice; the author, publisher, and Bloomberg L.P. cannot be held responsible for any loss incurred as a result of specific investments or planning decisions made by the reader.

First edition published 2009
1 3 5 7 9 10 8 6 4 2

Library of Congress Cataloging-in-Publication Data

Kamich, Bruce M.
    Chart patterns / Bruce M. Kamich.
        p. cm. – (Bloomberg market essentials)
    Includes bibliographical references and index.
    Summary: "Chart Patterns explains the essentials of one of the earliest and still most popular types of technical analysis, with details and basic trading strategies for the most important patterns. The book also includes practical guidance on how to recognize patterns in the difficult-to-decipher real-world charts"–Provided by publisher.
    ISBN 978-1-57660-300-0 (alk. paper)
    1. Stocks–Charts, diagrams, etc. 2. Financial futures–Charts, diagrams, etc. 3. Commodity futures–Charts, diagrams, etc. 4. Investment analysis. I. Title.

HG4638.K36 2009
332.63'2042–dc22   2009042833

Mixed Sources
Product group from well-managed forests,
controlled sources and recycled wood or fiber
www.fsc.org Cert no. SW-COC-000952
© 1996 Forest Stewardship Council
FSC

This book is dedicated to my wife, Susan, who I fall in love with all over again every time I see her.

Contents

Acknowledgments

MY FIRST ACKNOWLEDGEMENT goes to my wife, Susan, for her patience and support during this project. Setting up files and formatting word documents is not my strength, and Susan came to my rescue. My sons, Mark and Seth, also came to my assistance backing up files and saving my work off-site.

Regarding the start of this book, I want to thank Connie Brown for recommending me to Bloomberg Press and to Dan Nelson for allowing me to pursue this outside activity. Acknowledgement is also due to the staff at Bloomberg Press for its top-shelf editing job. As the book took shape, I needed charts, and Rich Escher, the president and chief executive officer of recognia (www.recognia.com), came to my aid. When I needed a layperson's understanding of a very complex math concept, I turned to Kris Kaufmann, president of Parallax Financial Research, Inc. (www.pfr.com), for his expert advice and council. Jonathan Arter of Taniscott Capital, Inc. sent me a copy of a hard-to-find book on long bases, and I know I would not have found it anywhere else. Steve Nison has been a friend for thirty-six years, and he would send me e-mails of encouragement when my energy level dropped.

Lastly, I must thank my first teacher of chart patterns and the art of technical analysis—Ralph Acampora. Without his inspiration, I would have taken an entirely different career path.

Introduction

EVERY BOOK STARTS with a germ of an idea. We read something, see something, or talk with friends and colleagues, and eventually, the proverbial light dawns. The initial idea grows and builds, and just sometimes, if we're lucky, maybe years later, a book emerges. At times, we stumble on this idea ourselves, and at other times, someone presents it to us. In spring 2007, I got a call from Stephen Isaacs, informing me that Bloomberg Press was interested in publishing a book about chart patterns. This book would be part of a series and would follow a book on Fibonacci analysis by Constance Brown; Connie had recommended me. I've known Connie for about twenty years and from her time working in New York. She is unique and very talented, so I felt right away that I was in good company. I gave the topic some thought, eventually worked up an outline, and things progressed from there.

Over the past fifteen years of teaching the subject of technical analysis, I have found that chart patterns are the most subjective part of this body of knowledge. Patterns are the part that most students and even professionals have problems mastering. From personal experience, I knew this was a worthwhile project, even if Bloomberg Press had not come up with the idea. In recent years, chart patterns and their interpretation have taken a back seat to many math-driven technical approaches, which seem easier to grasp and more clear-cut in terms of buy and sell signals and execution. The computer age has lead to a reliance on software to make our decisions.

Many books on technical analysis, including my first book, *How Technical Analysis Works* (New York Institute of Finance, 2003), try to span the whole subject from chart construction to patterns and indicators, and money management and tactics. Sometimes a book concentrates on one aspect, such as candlesticks or point-and-figure charting, but it has been a long time since a book has concentrated on just the classic vertical bar-chart patterns—and *only* the patterns. In addition to a concentration on patterns, I will also put some perspective on the past, the present, and just perhaps, the future of pattern recognition. Technicians believe that history tends to repeat itself, so a look back at the early days of charting can actually shed some light on the present and the future. The expression, "there is nothing new under the sun," might have its origins in the Bible (Ecclesiastes 1:9), but we should always strive to find a fresh slant on the most basic approaches.

CHAPTER 1

Why Study Patterns?

INVESTORS HAVE THE USE of many sophisticated tools to conduct research, trade, invest, track, and follow their holdings, and, of course, rebalance and maintain their investments. Why devote time and effort to study subjective and arcane chart patterns when high-powered methods of analysis, neural networks, and computer programs can pick stocks?

There are several reasons to study chart patterns. The first and probably most important one is that I and many other analysts and traders have found that these patterns cannot be random. I have been looking at charts of stock prices, commodities, and interest rates since the late 1960s. I believe that these patterns I have learned to recognize are the result of some very human behavior and not just "noise." These patterns repeat, just as history does. The human race has grown more intelligent and can process more and more information, but basic human nature has remained the same over the centuries. History is a reflection of and results from human nature—and price history is no different. When the stock market melted down in 2008, quantitative analysts and technical analysts looked back in history to find comparable periods: 1987, 1929, and even 1907 were brought out from the archives of charts and statistics.

Not convinced that human nature has been unchanged for centuries? Think about the stories in the Bible that keep repeating themselves thousands of years later, such as the struggle between brothers for the family inheritance, a woman wanting to be a mother, or a people who are enslaved—stories of greed, hope, and redemption. Or think about those famous Greek tragedies that seem to be playing out again in contemporary real life. The plays by William Shakespeare are hundreds of years old, yet the characters and plots are timeless. Isn't it amazing that these plays are still understood and people can relate to them today?

In 2007, the same old human emotion—*greed*—played a part in the markets, with private equity funds and hedge funds dominating the markets. And what about the stories of seemingly unlimited demand in China for goods and services ahead of the Olympics, and new stock market listings in Asia soaring to the stratosphere? Greed seemed to play a part again in the crude oil futures market as prices approached $147 per barrel and forecasters predicted $200, $250, and even $400 per barrel. The top in the U.S. stock market in 2007 was similar to the dot-com greed at the top in late 1999 and early 2000. Remember the summer of 2005? It seemed like nearly everyone from coast to coast and border to border was caught up in the ever-climbing real estate market. If one traveled overseas or looked at the "international listings" of real estate for sale, then one could see that the market for hot properties had gone global. In the first quarter of 2008, we witnessed *fear* as parts of the equity and credit markets plunged relentlessly into lows in January, and then again in March as the Wall Street firm Bear Stearns imploded. (See the Dow Jones Industrial Average index in **Figure 1.1**.)

Margin call liquidation, outright selling and fear of continuing losses drove the market down with only limited and temporary bouncebacks.

The end of Lehman Brothers shook people further, and the aftershocks continue to ripple around the world (see the Dow Jones Industrial Average index in **Figure 1.2**). Notice in **Figure 1.3** how quickly prices plunged after the loss of Lehman.

Prices sank to even lower in late 2008, with hedge funds imploding and people fearing a depression on the magnitude of the 1930s as stocks failed to hold at 10,000, and then 9,000 on the Dow.

The academic financial community has believed in the random walk theory since the early 1960s and has studies to support its theory, but more recent analyses of market data are increasingly pointing to an opposite conclusion. Professor Andrew Lo at the Sloan School of Management at the Massachusetts Institute of Technology has done

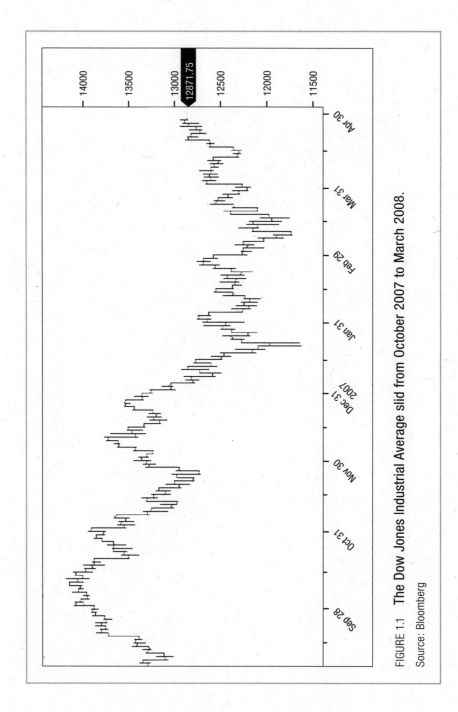

FIGURE 1.1 The Dow Jones Industrial Average slid from October 2007 to March 2008.

Source: Bloomberg

3

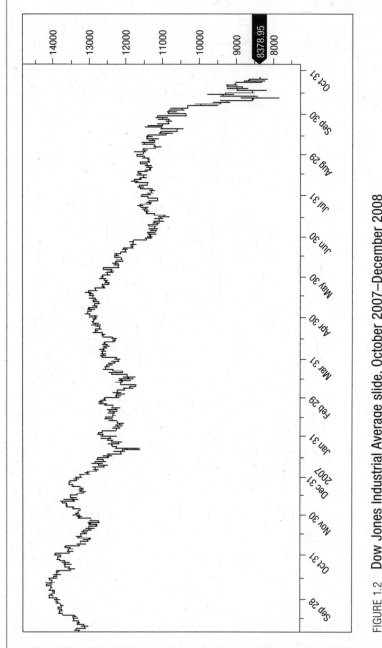

FIGURE 1.2 Dow Jones Industrial Average slide, October 2007–December 2008

Source: Bloomberg

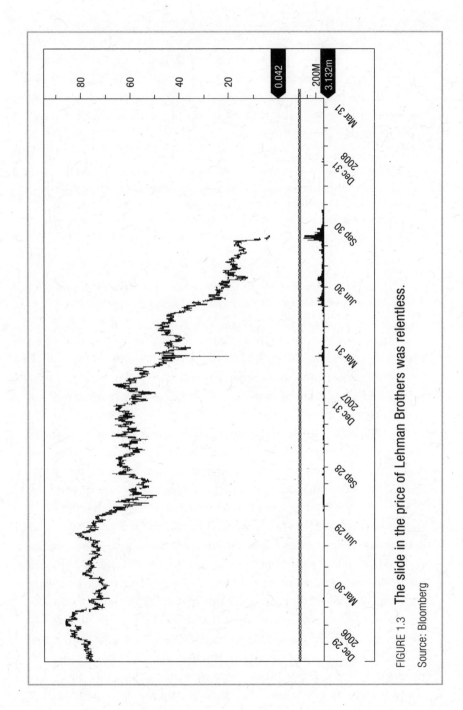

FIGURE 1.3   The slide in the price of Lehman Brothers was relentless.

Source: Bloomberg

5

extensive research into stock market behavior, which has shaken the pillars of the random walk and the efficient market belief system.[1] Another milestone in research supporting technical analysis was a paper by Dr. Carol Osler, now at Brandeis University, that was written while she was with the Research and Market Analysis Group of the Federal Reserve Bank of New York.[2] The abstract for the paper states, in part:

> This paper evaluates rigorously the predictive power of the head-and-shoulders pattern as applied to daily exchange rates. Though such visual, nonlinear chart patterns are applied frequently by technical analysts, our paper is one of the first to evaluate the predictive power of such patterns.

> Results:

> ... If one had speculated in all six currencies simultaneously, profits would have been both statistically and economically significant.

In midtown Manhattan, in Greenwich, Connecticut, and in other financial centers, legions of MBAs sit in front of computer terminals armed with algorithms and models to trade the markets, but can they "read" and anticipate the markets? Maybe. Can they judge one stock versus others? Perhaps. Can they understand the "personality" of the market that comes through the chart? I don't think so. There are many things that can influence stock prices, but many of them cannot be quantified—for example, an evaluation of management, market sentiment, and sociological and psychological factors. The more you look at factors that cannot be nailed down by hard numbers, the more you should look at the chart of the stock. The chart of the stock, index, or commodity reflects everyone's opinion about all factors—ones we can and cannot quantify. But the stock chart also gives a complete picture of a company's price history over any number of time spans. The chartist or technical analyst can see all this history at a glance. Can these bright graduates read beyond what they believe they can model? Do they ever get a "feel" for the markets and seem to be totally in sync like an athlete in "the zone"? At times, an accomplished chart reader can have a sixth sense about future price movements, just like an athlete who can sense an opponent's next move. Given the right math skills or computer programming background, pretty much anyone can build a trading model. If a new variable comes along, or if the importance of an old variable changes, the model probably won't adapt and will have to be refitted at some point. In an interview in the January 2009 issue of *Bloomberg Markets,* billionaire investor Wilbur Ross notes that computer risk models cannot replace good old real-world knowledge: "I think the real thing is not to confuse paper with what's the real world." You can't get more real than today's stock price.

The basic purpose of chart reading is to see the past history of a stock, judge the probable strength of demand and supply at various price levels, and predict the direction of prices. The clues to a stock's movement are recorded on the chart *if one takes the time to learn them.* When new variables come along, they show up in the price action right away; there is no need to go back and change formulas. I have a book in my office about neural networks with the subtitle *Gaining Predictive Edge in the Market.*[3] With nonlinear methods entrenched for more than a decade, the *new edge* in predicting and trading the markets should circle back to the early days of charting.

With so many traders and so much money going toward black-box systems and sophisticated math-driven programs to get their "edge," one can easily believe that the real edge is now reverting back, in part, to the "old-school ways" that Wilbur Ross might endorse. One can easily see the bias toward indicators, math and back testing by the kinds of articles in the popular industry magazines, the seminars for the public, and various webinars today. I find it interesting that in other areas of life, there is a return by successful practitioners to the older, hands-on methods of doing things. For example, artists in the kitchen have returned to old ways of cooking, baking and preparing food in reaction to the mass-produced and heavily processed foods of today. A number of the popular chefs today have spent time learning from authentic cooks and butchers in Tuscany or in small villages in France, for example. The *New York Times* "Dining & Wine" section has reported on artists' collectives in Brooklyn, New York, where people are making pickles, cheeses and chocolates by hand. There are a number of art colonies around the country where you can find craftspeople returning to their roots or their grandparents' roots to make musical instruments, furniture, rugs, and even canoes.

Chart reading takes a bit of intuition and the belief that these patterns actually work. This belief should be based on experience; seeing these patterns work in real time is learning by example. In my undergraduate course on technical analysis, I make all my students maintain a bar chart of a stock every day for the semester. The personal construction of a chart keeps them in touch with the market's fluctuations and can convince them in real time that formations like flags and pennants really work, although this may need to be pointed out to them the first few times.

Intuition isn't something one can teach, but the prepared mind can be trained to be more intuitive. By looking at enough charts and patterns, my students become like the original ticker tape watchers back in the early 1900s who could not escape the tape. Traders eighty years ago studied the bid or offer quote for each security they followed and the tape action with the volume behind each trade. These tape watchers could sense when a stock was under accumulation. They looked for a stock that rallied on one thousand shares and fell on a few hundred. Seeing a stock advance on increased volume and decline on lighter volume is how tape readers decided on what stocks to buy. Retail traders were still reading the tape in the 1960s and early 1970s, but tape watchers drifted away from the boardrooms of brokerage houses when someone decided the ticker tape was an unnecessary expense. When the ticker tape disappeared, the account executives (as they were called back then) got the New York Stock Exchange tape streaming on their desktops. Because professional money management has replaced individual stock picking, account executives have become advisers, and the advice has changed.

Although the tape can still be seen on CNBC or Bloomberg Television, the skills of the tape reader have disappeared. Some day-trading firms have tried to bring this skill back with the detailed reading of market-maker quotes. When everyone else in your firm or on the Street is programming and searching on a computer for patterns and intermarket relationships in the data, and they get away from *seeing* patterns, a return to this approach could give you a real edge. Today, more than ever, I believe the person who can look at the market in the old way can learn to outperform others in this formula-driven market.

It may seem strange, but observing is really a skill to be developed and honed with experience. Law officers, doctors and others are often trained to be better observers. The experienced, senior police officers in each precinct teach the rookies on the job to study people and size up situations. Teaching hospitals do, in fact, teach interns to look at the patient and observe subtle details in skin and nail color, reflexes, and so on, in addition to running all those annoying and expensive tests. Experience on the job will also teach most people more than what can come from textbooks and the classroom. So why not Wall Street traders? Empirical experience is better, in my opinion, than browsing the Internet or using pattern-recognition software or some database of patterns. By looking at more and more charts, training your eyes to identify the patterns, and subsequently seeing what develops, you can cultivate the skill and art of chart reading. Finding a confusing or questionable pattern and discussing it with a more experienced chart reader or technical mentor should also help the process. The technical analysts who were at the top of their game in the 1970s and 1980s had spent many years looking at charts and developing indicators by hand. Keeping advance–decline data and hundreds of charts up to date with a No. 2 pencil day after day gives a depth of experience that you don't get from preloaded software and spreadsheets. Natural talent always helps, but expertise in any field comes with a significant amount of hard work. Successful chart reading should be no different.

From my experience, the financial press doesn't really know about, doesn't recognize, and certainly doesn't respect, chart patterns or, for that matter, the broader subject of technical analysis. Financial reporters and their editors need a basic fundamental story today to explain today's price movements—never understanding that prices discount events and people anticipate the news very often. A good reporter may actually put his finger on some piece of news that some investors may be focused on today, but he or she may not touch on factors that might be in the back of investors' minds, or on their fears or hopes, which also move prices. Investors are human and not totally rational when it comes to the buying and selling of securities and other products. We think we may know what moves markets and people, but as Richard W. Schabacker said in the preface to his book *Stock Market Theory and Practice* (New York: B.C. Forbes Publishing Company, 1930), "of paramount importance, however, for our own consideration, is the ultimate fact that no adviser, no theory, no amount of experience, can approach infallibility." And this seems very true nearly eighty years later: knowing chart patterns in addition to all the tools you may have learned in graduate school gives you an edge, because only a handful of schools and instructors have been brave enough to teach technical analysis. With technical analysis being taught in perhaps only twenty or so schools across the United States and Canada, you can feel pretty confident that thousands of newly minted finance majors and MBAs are not trading with the added information gained from charts.

Charts patterns have fanciful, unscientific names, but you shouldn't be confused or put off by technical analysis jargon, such as head and shoulders, double tops, triangles, and island reversal patterns. All of these patterns—in fact, all patterns—are based on the simple tenets of support, resistance, and trend. All of this will become easier to understand as you make your way through the following chapters. You may have read many other books on technical analysis including chart patterns and may wonder what can be learned from yet another book on the subject. I have found that no matter how many books I have read on the subject of technical analysis, I can and do find something new and worthwhile with each new author who has been able to articulate things a little differently.

Will years of study make you a great investor or trader? In all honesty, I cannot guarantee it. Technical analysis has been around more than 120 years in the United States, but it still is not as widespread as fundamental analysis, which started around 1934 when corporate balance sheets became credible. I once read somewhere that if studying the history of the market was the only thing you needed to be a great technician, then librarians would be very rich. Will a study of chart patterns improve your odds of making money? I think so, provided you use the patterns along with a strong dose of money management and discipline.

From 1900–1920, the number of published patterns was actually fewer, or perhaps analysts and traders back then just kept things simpler. Looking at the few stock market books from the era that have survived, there were seven major accumulation and distribution patterns and just five continuation patterns. The seven key patterns from the 1920s were the head and shoulders, the common turn (rounded), the triangle (symmetrical), the bottom (triangle), the double bottom and top, the complex bottom (multiple head and shoulders) and the broadening pattern. The gaps were the breakaway and the exhaustion, but not the runaway gap. They also described the common gap, which is not considered meaningful today.

In the past, the chart was just a memory aid. One could not depend on a mental picture of an individual stock or the various market averages. Few are blessed with a photographic memory. The chart was the way to see at a glance the stock's price history, regardless of whether you had it under personal observation or not. Years ago, you really couldn't trade actively without a chart. The chart was needed to gauge entry and exit points to determine price targets and timing. I think it is the same way today, and so do many others. But charts shouldn't be used alone, no matter how much you might come to trust and rely on the chart. Even a dyed-in-the-wool technician like me believes you should understand the fundamentals of the instrument under consideration. There is no 100-percent guaranteed perfect approach to investing, so a blending of methods should yield superior results.

CHAPTER NOTES

1. I encourage you to read *A Non-Random Walk Down Wall Street* by Andrew W. Lo and A. Craig MacKinlay (Princeton, NJ: Princeton University Press, 1999).

2. For a published version of this report, see Kevin P. H. Chang and Carol Osler, "Methodical Madness: Technical Analysis and the Irrationality of Exchange-Rate Forecasts," *Economic Journal* 109(458) (October 1999): 636–661.

3. Paul D. McNelis, *Neural Networks in Finance: Gaining Predictive Edge in the Market* (Burlington, MA: Elsevier Academic Press, 2005).

CHAPTER 2

The Past
1910–1960

TODAY, TRADERS AND INVESTORS have access to faster and faster computers and more sophisticated software to help find new patterns in stock charts, and between asset classes, currencies, and commodities. We can also use sophisticated neural networks to try to anticipate turns in the markets. We also have lots of help today in creating and back testing trading systems, but what did traders and analysts have to work with back in 1880, 1900, or the 1920s?

Some traders probably worked on the back of an envelope—literally. This was the early beginning of the point and figure method. Working in Smith Barney's legendary chart room, I found a chart book from 1941 published by M.C. Horsey & Company. The copy was the twentieth edition and published monthly, so this service apparently began at the end of 1939. There were chart services available before that day, but nothing before that date survived at Smith Barney. I tried to find out what might have been published in the 1920s, but unfortunately, the technicians and analysts who were in the business in the 1920s, such as John Schultz and others, have passed on.

The Horsey chart service billed itself as the largest portfolio of stock charts ever published, so this might imply that other services published smaller portfolios. These charts were monthly range charts that showed only the high and low for the month, but they did not show the close of the month. This service also did not show the monthly volume along the bottom of the chart, even though other early charts displayed the volume of shares traded. In his 1930 book, *Stock Market*

Theory and Practice, R. W. Schabacker makes note of the Graphic Market Record of New York City; this enterprise published a set of charts daily or weekly with ranges and volume of sales. Periodicals such as the *Commercial & Financial Chronicle* and the *Annalist* published daily ranges. Schabacker recommended that investors maintain their own charts if they had the time. He believed that an individual could not trade intelligently without them and that they should not be used alone. Charts could be started easily from scratch and should be taken back at least three months, if possible. Traders would have to visit the public library and go through the daily newspapers to get the complete data of highs, lows, closes, and volume to make the bar chart. Schabacker did not consider the opening price to be particularly important, and to keep things simpler, he did not include it.

An even older charting approach than bar charts is the *book method of charting,* referred to in a 1901 editorial in the *Wall Street Journal* by Charles Henry Dow. Book method charts were plotted from the ticker tape, which was also known as the *market book.* In an 1898 pamphlet by Hoyle (a pseudonym), *The Game in Wall Street, and How to Play It Successfully* (originally published in New York by J. S. Ogilvie Publishing Co., 1898, and reprinted in 1968 by Fraser Publishing Co. in Burlington, Vermont) he refers to *fluctuation records,* but did not give the method a name. By 1903, the book method became known as *figure charts,* according to *The Definitive Guide to Point and Figure* by Jeremy du Plessis (Petersfield, Hampshire, UK: Harriman House, 2005).

In the early days, when charts had to be done by hand, a trader could only follow so many stocks, and it was easier to do a daily bar chart than to create weekly and monthly charts. Creating weekly and monthly charts obviously required collecting and tabulating a large volume of data without the help of today's spreadsheets. Technical tools have always been the result of the data available and the imagination and creativity of individuals. When I started in the securities business in 1973, the commodity consulting firm I worked for was using chart paper from the Keuffel and Esser Company (known as K&E for short). The drafting company was founded in 1867 by German immigrants William J. D. Keuffel and Herman Esser. The firm of Keuffel and Esser started out in New York and sold drawing materials, such as specialized papers and drafting supplies. Although there were commercial chart services in the 1970s for the common futures contracts, by and large, if you had to follow particular cash commodity markets and any "off the run" Treasury security, you did so by hand. I still remember the commercial artist employed at my first job, whose job was to draw cash commodity charts of things like No. 2 yellow corn, soybean meal, heavy native hides, and palm oil prices. Charts of these cash commodities were not in great enough demand by the public to warrant a commercial service, and even in 1976, collecting their data and drawing them by hand was the only way to maintain them.

Typically, books about charting and technical analysis assume that supply and demand drive all chart patterns. One could take that as fact and not go any further, but it is important to acknowledge that human emotions—greed and fear—can also impact chart patterns, especially at tops and bottoms. Beyond supply and demand and human emotions, we can also consider what I call *institutional factors*. In 2009, technicians are wrestling with changes, such as bans on shorting and the elimination of the uptick rule. Decades ago, pools were the institutional factor that affected the chart patterns. Pools were not all that much different from hedge funds. Pool operators had concentrations of capital from wealthy individuals, as do hedge funds today or the commodity pool operators in the 1970s and 1980s. Pools were in their heyday in the late 1920s in the United States. Pools often had written agreements among a group of investors who delegated trading authority to one manager to trade a specific stock for a specified time and then divide the profits or losses. The triangle or coil pattern was considered the definitive sign of a pool operation underway. The triangle formation (see Chapter 6) has prices moving back and forth in broad swings. The pool operator would get most of his buying or selling done in those broad swings. As the triangle moves toward its apex, the swings up and down are shorter, and the pool can clean up or accumulate the remaining supply at a bottom. Or the pool can sell and distribute the rest of its holdings near a top.

I looked at a few books that have survived from that early era and found there were just seven bar-chart patterns and some point-and-figure patterns. In Schabacker's book cited earlier, there were nearly one hundred books noted in the bibliography with publication dates from 1848 to 1928. Only a handful of the titles of those books suggest that they had anything to do with speculation that actually might include charting or technical analysis. Despite this absence of published material, I seriously doubt that analysts and traders ninety or a hundred years ago were not talented or imaginative enough to find more than seven patterns; instead, this suggests that time was limited. If traders had more time to observe more charts, then perhaps they could have found and named more patterns. Commercially produced charts like H. M. Horsey Charts got started in the late 1930s, while Standard Statistics and Poor's Publishing did work in the 1920s, so one might assume that charts were largely hand drawn before the 1920s. If you were active in the stock market in those early years, drawing your own charts was desirable because it kept you in constant touch with the marketplace and the daily jiggles or fluctuations. If you had to spend most of your day maintaining charts by hand, it left very little time for analysis and study. If you found a few things that seemed to work more often than not, then it would be understandable that that would suffice. I think people do that even today.

The seven basic patterns during the 1920s were given the following names:

1. the head and shoulders bottom and top,
2. the common upward turn and downward turn (the rounding bottom and top),
3. the triangle bottom and top (what we would call the *symmetrical triangle* today),
4. the ascending bottom and top (or the *triangle* of today),
5. the double bottom and top,
6. the complex bottom or top (or the *complex head-and-shoulders* pattern), and
7. the broadening top and bottom (which today we see as both a *reversal* pattern and sometimes a *continuation* pattern)

In *Technical Analysis and Stock Market Profits* (1932), Schabacker devoted more attention to the technical approach and outlined most of the technical patterns we use today.

In the 1940s and 1950s, analysts such as Robert Edwards and John Magee added other top and bottom formations, dormant bottoms and scallops, three kinds of triangles, other reversals and more gaps. In the classic book, *Technical Analysis of Stock Trends* (fourth ed.) (Boston: J. Magee, 1957), John Magee comments on "modern versus old-style markets": "We have mentioned in our discussion of formations that some of them have appeared less frequently in charts of the past ten years than they did in prior years, and others more frequently" (Magee, p. 186). Magee felt there were reasons for these changes, such as Securities and Exchange Commission (SEC) regulations, higher margin requirements, a greater level of sophistication of the public, among others. There is little proof or support of these reasons outside of the SEC regulations of the day, which tracked the purchases and sales of officers and directors and largely stopped some of the manipulation in the markets. Magee was a skeptic, viewing the release and timing of company news as a tool used by insiders for their own personal purposes. In his book, Magee referred to the old-time "plunger," who hadn't disappeared in the 1950s and 1960s. The famous Jessie Livermore was known as the "Boy Plunger," even when he was no longer a young boy trying his hand in the bucket shops in Boston when he was 15. (Livermore had youthful good looks and placed large bucket shop bets, hence the nickname.) The plunger, regardless of his age, took on large stock positions. Today, we might think of some aggressive hedge fund managers and traders as plungers using extreme amounts of leverage to bully the markets and make their "bear raids" or "bull raids."

Magee's observations of fifty years ago are very similar to today's complaints about the market being too difficult to trade or understand, with hedge funds seemingly amplifying moves and having greater leverage, and the elimination of the uptick rule by the SEC changing the way trading is done. Various market watchers like technical analysts and some fund managers note the rise of exchange-traded funds and the disappearance of volume from the floor influencing chart patterns. It is not just technical analysts who suggest that these changes have contributed to the way the markets operate and the resulting chart patterns one must interpret. Speaking to many financial advisers (brokers) on a daily basis, I find that they are often stumped by the seemingly daily two hundred to three hundred Dow point swings in the market.

In the early 1960s, commodity analysts, such as William Jiler, talked about line and saucer formations, V formations, coils, box patterns, drift patterns, and bull and bear traps. In the late 1960s, trading stocks in high school, I read the work of technical analyst Ken Ward of Reynolds & Company. The analysis was simple, well-reasoned and aimed at the public, which, oddly enough, was more comfortable with the markets and buying and selling individual securities than many people are today. The mutual fund industry certainly existed in the 1960s; I remember overhearing dinner party conversations about how my parents' friends bought and sold stocks, corporate bonds, and even some preferred stocks. Balance sheets were not as complicated, and people did, in fact, read and understand them. My late Uncle Sid was a businessman and taught me to read these sheets when I was thirteen. Reports from brokerage houses were written clearly, and the disclaimers were shorter than the reports! Currency translations did not matter, and we did not need to account for inflation.

In the 1970s, 1980s, and part of the 1990s, more attention was paid to creating and using math-based indicators than chart patterns, and chart reading took a back seat. Traders and analysts were busy creating indicators like the relative strength index, stochastics, the moving average convergence divergence oscillator, and various moving averages. The next time chart reading became important was in the early 1990s with the "discovery" of Japanese candlestick charts. Even though Japanese candlesticks had been in use for more than two hundred years in Japan, they were unknown in the United States until my friend Steve Nison popularized them here in the 1990s.

CHAPTER 3

The Present

IN THE TECHNICAL ANALYSIS classes I teach at Baruch College in New York in the evening, I have observed over several semesters that many—and sometimes most—students have serious trouble with chart patterns. One might think that young undergrads have open minds and are quick learners, that they are not biased by years of "fundamental brain washing," and that these students would pick up pattern recognition quickly. These may be logical assumptions, but over the last sixteen years, the truth has been something different. First, and surprisingly, I have found that some students see patterns where they really don't exist. On multiple-choice exams where there is a possible answer of "none of the above," students usually don't have a problem making that selection if it's true, but there seems to be some uncontrolled desire to mark charts with patterns that appear like nothing in the textbooks. The "pattern" they mark might be upside down, inverted, or way too small to be a *major* top or bottom. Second, I find that even bright students have trouble training their minds to find patterns. Chart reading is a skill to be developed and honed, and the more one does it, the better one gets. Rather than really working at being a good chart reader, most students gravitate to the popular math-based indicators for buy and sell signals. Although my class is filled with eighty eager students each semester, they have already heard from a number of professors that charts do not have prediction value and that markets move on fundamentals. After fourteen weeks, they generally come to respect the analysis of past price behavior and any clues it can shed on the future.

Even when students find the correctly shaped chart pattern, they often apply them in the wrong way. They might have the wrong location, such as outlining a rising or ascending triangle in a downtrend. Or they see an incorrect volume pattern in a hoped-for head-and-shoulders top formation—increasing or flat volume through the pattern instead of decreasing through the shoulders and head (more on this in Chapter 4). Or they have found a double top, but what they are looking at is too small a pattern in terms of time to be considered a major top pattern. I see these mistakes both from undergraduate and graduate students.

Professional traders and analysts regularly make these same mistakes. (During October 2008, many market observers talked about an equilateral triangle on the Dow Jones Industrial Average (DJIA) that was poised to break out to the downside. Of course, when too many people look for something to happen, it typically doesn't happen.) **Figure 3.1** shows the potential bearish chart pattern nearly everyone saw, but the actual result is shown in **Figure 3.2**.

Even experienced professionals can find patterns problematic at times. For example, a colleague was preparing to make a presentation to

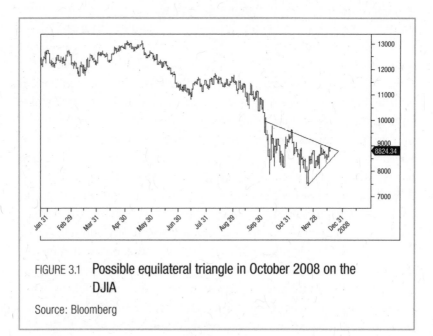

FIGURE 3.1   **Possible equilateral triangle in October 2008 on the DJIA**

Source: Bloomberg

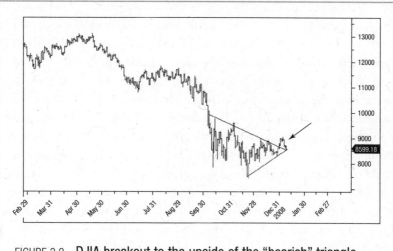

FIGURE 3.2 **DJIA breakout to the upside of the "bearish" triangle**

Source: Bloomberg

an office in Maryland. The presentation was to be part current market outlook and part tutorial. In looking for some real-life or live examples of patterns, we both found it difficult to find a perfectly clear textbook head-and-shoulders top pattern with the correct volume pattern. Looking back at either the 1999–2000 period or the 2007 top, we were adamant that there were plenty of top patterns to choose from, but getting everything to look completely accurate was actually hard. With hindsight, we easily found the correctly shaped patterns that "worked" really well, but without the confirming volume. Maybe this is the future of patterns? The shape of the price pattern will be all-important, and the consideration of volume as a confirming indicator will be ignored.

What has happened to chart books? Twenty years ago, many trad-ers and analysts would have sets of charts (NYSE, AMEX, NAS-DAQ) delivered at home on Saturday or at the office early Monday. The analysts who got a set of charts on the weekend would page through them, looking for interesting patterns and trends to high-light to brokers, salespeople, and traders on Monday, or to put on a short list for further research. Only very few of the older—or shall we say, "seasoned"—analysts do this anymore. The vast majority of people have set up computer programs to search for price and volume patterns, and then have those signals pushed to them as e-mail alerts or by some other delivery system. The number of people still subscribing to chart books has been in a serious downtrend for years and probably hasn't hit bottom. Naturally, the next step is for these few remaining chart book companies to close their doors as the budget cuts from the 2007–2009 bear market take their toll on expenses. Although chart books have essentially faded from the landscape, an abundance of choices exist online. One Web site I use for three-box point-and-figure charts also offers candlestick charts, line charts, and open-high, low-close bar charts. Other sites or software packages offer traditional one-box reversals, Gann swing charts and Equivolume charts. One of the firms skillful at identifying patterns is recognia (www.recognia.com) in western Canada. Another firm, Parallax Financial Research, Inc. (www.pfr.com), is known for its innovative financial methods with chaos and complexity theory. I have used its work extensively for market timing for more than fifteen years, even though I admit I have a very weak background in math and no experience in mathematical modeling.

For perhaps twenty or twenty-five years, mathematical indicators have been easily used largely in place of chart patterns. Instead of learning to read supply and demand through price patterns, which have a longer learning curve, traders want to use buy and sell tools quickly. Most of these indicators are coincident with market turns such as the relative strength index (RSI). Many of the indicators, such as moving averages, lag the market, and a few indicators actually lead the market—for example, momentum and rate of change. In reality, most people actually don't apply most of these mathematical indicators well. They look at the indicator, which is a derivative of the price action, and they largely ignore the price action. In contrast, I recommend looking at the price action closely, because this is the real thing you buy and sell. There seems to be more faith in math indicators that may have a shorter learning curve and reliance on software than subjective pattern recognition, which improves with experience and is an acquired skill. I have often seen traders sell, acting on an overbought signal, just as the stock is breaking out of a multimonth consolidation! Why are they selling just when they really should be buying more of this very strong stock, which is only overbought on a daily scale? A stock that goes up when it is considered overbought is a strong stock and should be bought and not sold. An overbought stock is really strong. If it stays overbought, it is likely to go higher as the demand does not fall off at the higher price levels.

Other chart pattern problems lie in creating or seeing patterns that aren't there. Letting a pattern play out to completion is frustrating—we want to get in early and make more money and a higher return, but this can sometimes lead to "jumping the gun" or "jumping the pattern." If you always try to finish the sentences of your spouse, for example, you'll at some point assume something very wrong or put your own biases into the answer and be wrong anyway! The same idea can be true with patterns. A rush to capitalize on what seems to be a small double-top pattern might actually be a bullish rectangle continuation pattern that hasn't yet completely formed. If you go short anticipating the double top to break much lower only to find that the bullish rectangle breaks out to the upside, then you could quickly give up on or swear off chart patterns.

The volume that should confirm the price pattern has become a significant problem in 2009. With volume disappearing from the trading floors and exchanges and into dark pools, for example, I am willing to suggest that price will be even more important in pattern recognition in the years ahead. Oddly, history may be coming full circle in that the chart books from the 1930s do not display the volume below the chart. In the 1930s, we did not have the data collection and spreadsheet capabilities of today to follow weekly and monthly volume stock by stock. We might also find nowadays that patterns may also be changing, because it is estimated that half to three-quarters of all trading volume in listed stocks is now being executed by quantitative programs and algorithmic formula trading. These programs can generate rapid price movements as all the similar programs on Wall Street kick in. This shouldn't be a surprise: the designers of these programs had similar financial engineering courses at top schools and they wind up developing similar programs. Volume might expand when the programs perceive the same thing in the marketplace, as opposed to tape watchers and chartists watching a pattern develop and then anticipating or acting on the breakout at different points, depending on their time horizon and risk tolerance.

Today we should consider chart patterns as insurance for fundamental analysis, as analyst Ken Tower has said on occasion at seminars and lectures on college campuses. Often a stock will weaken before negative news has been released and bottom ahead of improving news. Imagine being able to find stocks that are just beginning to start an advance, instead of reading about stocks that have doubled and are now being upgraded to a "strong buy" or "outperform." Would you like to be able to identify the next group to which the stock market's attention and money are rotating? The skill of analyzing supply and demand in simple price charts is really all it takes. The craft of reading charts and the science of technical analysis have been used to evaluate and trade various securities in this country for more than 120 years, but most investors have little in-depth knowledge and typically shun these tools, even though they can add so much to one's investment success.

"Buy the rumor and sell the news" is an old Wall Street adage that holds a lot of truth. Just look at the rallies in bond prices ahead of the numerous interest rates cuts by the Federal Reserve Board in the past three years. Bonds have rallied on the expectation of a cut and then declined or traded sideways when the news was announced. Technicians believe that the markets discount the future—that the markets are forward looking. The current news about a company may be negative, but the price action of the stock of the firm may be showing that better times lie ahead by six to nine months. "A stock may look good on the chart well before the fundamentals have really improved. Investigate the ones with good bases and cull out the ones that don't have improving numbers," Kenneth Garvey, a long-time Wall Street money manager, once told me.

Have you ever read a headline on a business story like "Stocks Rally Despite Earnings Disappointments"? This is an example of how markets and people are looking ahead to the next quarter or beyond. Remember that nothing in the investment world is guaranteed, but blending a bullish chart picture with a developing turnaround in the company's fundamental numbers is more likely to put you on the road to success. It doesn't matter how you begin—scan for good companies and then look at the chart or scan the charts for promising bases (see Chapter 5). Then examine the fundamental story.

CHAPTER 4

Major Tops

WHEN I BEGIN TEACHING students or financial market professionals about chart patterns, I always start with the major top formations. (The top is not necessarily the highest price level reached by a security but actually a process in which ownership of a company's shares shifts from strong hands or owners to weak hands.) An examination of major tops also must include a brief discussion of the major bottoms, or when the ownership shifts from weak hands or owners to strong hands. I then work down to the various short- and intermediate-term continuation patterns. Once the basic patterns are covered, I drill down to the "nonpatterns" of gaps, and finally, one-day, two-day, and island reversals. If you learn only one pattern really well, though, you absolutely must know how to identify a major top before getting involved with the various shorter time-frame patterns and reversals.

If you can recognize the major tops, then you have a better chance of avoiding the big declines that lie out there. Imagine doing really well in your trading account and making a lot of money with the various short-term patterns, but then losing the bulk of your profits by missing the major top and riding a winner to a big loser. I suspect by the time the bear market that began in October 2007 is finished, more investors and advisers will wish they had paid attention to the major tops that formed in 2007. Indeed, the old texts often started their discussion of important formations with the head-and-shoulders pattern, or a top with three rally attempts with the middle rally being higher, the best known of all top patterns.

One thing to keep in mind when investing or trading is that you can have only five results whenever you buy or sell any security: a small loss, a small gain, a scratch (basically, a transaction in which you enter and exit at the same price), a large loss, and a large gain. Over time and with a lot of transactions or back-testing observations, the sum of the small gains and small losses and scratches will tend to even themselves out. If you can recognize the major top patterns and take the appropriate defensive market action, then you should be able to avoid that awful account-closing major loss and wind up with the very desirable large gain—*if* you do everything right.

Major tops are just that: they are *major* formations of prices and psychology with the emphasis on the word *major*. Ideally, these take place over several months—perhaps nine months to well over a year or more. For example, the major tops in Freddie Mac (**Figure 4.1**) and Fannie Mae (**Figure 4.2**) go all the way back to 1997. The tops were large, and the resulting declines were swift and crushing.

Freddie Mac shows a massive top developing from 1998 until it started to break down decisively in late 2006. Notice how it took only one year to wipe out the gains of nearly two decades. This

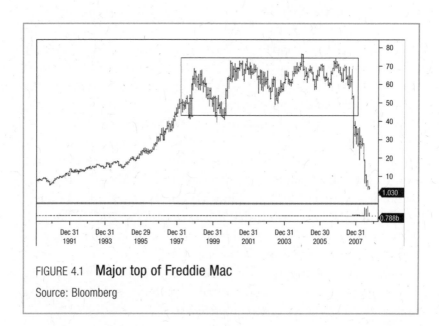

FIGURE 4.1   **Major top of Freddie Mac**

Source: Bloomberg

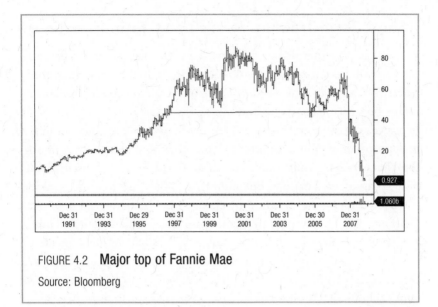

FIGURE 4.2 **Major top of Fannie Mae**

Source: Bloomberg

is a good example of why I start the study of chart patterns with major tops.

The chart of Fannie Mae shows a ten-year top pattern that reversed the 100 times price appreciation of the prior twenty years. Once this stock broke down from the top pattern, the decline was relentless. Ignoring the breakdown was hazardous to your wealth!

Many major top formations are still playing out on the downside in 2009, not quite two years since the top. A large well-run company typically doesn't sink quickly—although we can probably all think of some companies whose fortunes reversed sharply from a lost lawsuit or serious product recall, a new competitor, or a change in the laws or regulations affecting their industries. But usually, it takes several quarters or longer for a company's momentum to erode. Time is needed to slip from top dog to underdog. In addition to the time needed to see a firm lose its competitive edge and for earnings or revenues to peak, we also need time for the large shareholders to distribute the shares they acquired at the last major cycle low for this stock. *Distribution* is typically done as expertly as the *accumulation* of the stock.

Short-Term Trading Versus Long-Term Investing

Traders and investors will probably make use of chart patterns differently, but this will not change the pattern, only the way they might use these patterns. When I use the word *trader*, I am not talking about people who might buy on the opening and sell in the afternoon or by the close of trading. In my mind, a trader is someone who is looking to catch a one-, two-, or even four-month move in the price of a security. Short-term day traders could make use of some patterns discussed in this book that appear intraday, but more likely, they are looking to trade based on order flow or some mechanical or mathematical approach. I believe there are many investors who are probably focused on a twelve- to eighteen-month time-frame and should be making use of many of the chart patterns in this book, especially the major tops and bottoms. If you are looking to be an investor in stocks, bonds, or commodities for a major move of a year or two, then you need to pay attention to the major tops and bottoms to help shift the odds in your favor. As analysts or investors, we may have discovered a compelling fundamental story, but combining that story with a major bottom pattern will only improve your chances of making money in the markets. The trader might consider shorting a stock breaking down from a major top formation while investors might avoid that same security as they want to position the stock from the long side at some time in the future. There should be no negative stigma in being a trader and no unrealistic positive attitude toward being an investor. Chart patterns are there to be used by any and all regardless of the time-frame in which they want to operate.

To understand the creation of tops, we must first explore bottoms, or market declines, when prices are near their lowest, but we need to remember that a bottom is a pattern and not necessarily the lowest price. Let's think about what is going on at a bottom. At an important stock market bottom, the public has typically given up on trying to make money in equities. Fear of loss and bearish news reports are the order of the day. One sign of disinterest is that few are interested in buying an initial public offering. Cash and treasuries are considered the best assets to hold. At a bottom, typically, only a seasoned long-term investor will look beyond the recession or see

In the 1920s, it was common to refer to investors as either *short-swing traders* or *long-swing operators*—or *short-term traders* and *long-term investors* in today's terms. The long-swing operators would *accumulate* a position (or purchase a "line" as they called it) on a scale down. For example, a 10-percent position might be taken at entry and then 10 percent more when the stock fell $3, $4, $5, or even $10. These operators would buy into weakness and could accumulate stock without paying up and pushing the stock higher on expanding volume. Large stock operators tried to hide their activities and did not want to alert tape watchers and anyone else to their intentions. Bearish stories might be circulated on the floor or a reporter might be taken to lunch and fed a bearish story. The subsequent negative story in the press might "shake out" some holders of the stock, allowing the operators to buy even more stock at favorable prices. Once these pool operators accumulated their full position or line, they would try to influence other reporters to write a bullish story on the company.

across the current problems of the company to buy shares when they are "undervalued." These long-term investors are typically the only people who will buy in the late stages of a serious market decline. "Valuation" is not normally in the vocabulary of most technical analysts because it usually involves metrics of a fundamental basis and tools they are not familiar with. (Technicians generally believe that the learning curve for a competent fundamental analyst is fairly long and doesn't usually translate over or migrate easily to other industries. Chartists generally like the idea of being an instant expert in anything they can get a chart on—just one glance and we can decide if we want to be bullish or bearish—no need for mind-bending fundamental analysis.) The long-term investor will look to buy undervalued securities when short-term traders might be discouraged and selling.

I once learned what I believe is a very valuable lesson from a partner and senior technical analyst at a major buy-side firm that managed hundreds of billions of dollars in Boston. This gentleman took me aside over lunch and in a fatherly way told me that perhaps only 5 percent of the investing population really does its homework and truly understands the fundamentals of an industry or a sector, whether these people work in the industry or study it as buy-side or sell-side analysts. Another 10 percent of the population, he said, follows the 5 percent—these are the tape watchers, people who read 13Ds (beneficial ownership reports), follow insider transactions, floor brokers, and technical analysts. The other 85 percent of the population really doesn't have a clue what is going on, according to this analyst. Thus, you want to watch what the top analysts are doing and what they are accumulating because they have done their homework. One way to do this is to look at the prospectus of some of the specialized industry mutual funds and see what positions are being increased. Having a stock in their portfolio tells you they have vetted it in various fundamental screens, but an increase in the position tells you they are growing more confident about that particular stock's prospects.

Short-term traders are motivated by price and the trend, and in a mature down trend, they will either short or stand aside with their dollars or euros in a money market fund or T-bills. Investors, however, tend to be motivated more by price and value, and they will use weakness in the marketplace to a build a long position in stocks that they consider undervalued. This is why you want to watch what the buy-side analysts are doing—part of that 5 percent. As technicians, we want to follow the clues in price and volume left behind from those investors who have been quietly buying stock near the bottom when nearly everyone else was bearish. At a major top, we also want to pay attention when these investors turn sellers of their now over-valued securities.

What to Look For

The key ingredients we should be looking for to give us confidence that we have correctly identified a major top are:

- location,
- shape,
- time,

- having something to reverse,
- breaking a major up-trend line and probably the 200-day moving average line,
- volume, and
- sometimes news about the company and the general economy.

This seems like a lot to master, so we'll take each point separately.

Location

If you ask people involved in real estate, "What are the three most important things in real estate?", the answer is always, "Location, location, location!"

The same is true of major tops. Finding a top pattern—whether a head and shoulders or double top, as we will soon cover in detail—should make sense. We shouldn't be looking for a major top in a stock trading around $10 per share, but rather at something like $110 per share. At $110, we have a stock at a relatively high price level and something to reverse. There will be occasional exceptions; for example, we may find a uranium stock or a very junior gold miner that has rallied from five or ten cents on the Vancouver Stock Exchange (VSE) to $10 or $12, and this will look just as extended and dramatic as a stock that has gone from $10 to $120. At $10, we could easily have a $5 decline or a 50-percent retracement, but the idea of a major top at $10 seems a bit of a stretch, at least to me. In June 2007, the price of uranium ran up to around $138 per pound, and some junior names soared from just a few pennies to over $4 (see **Figure 4.3**), and the tops were only two months in duration.

The chart in Figure 4.3 of JNR Resources (JNN) listed on the VSE breaks out of a ten-year base formation in "pennies" before a one-and-a-half-year rally and an inverted-V top pattern.

Shape

In the following paragraphs and other chapters we will discuss the shape of the various chart patterns. The shape of the pattern represents the result of the buying and selling of many different traders and investors; this

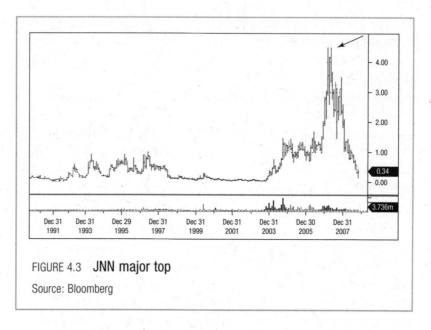

FIGURE 4.3   **JNN major top**

Source: Bloomberg

is a visual representation of supply and demand. The shapes described
will be more like the ideal pattern, but things are rarely ideal in real life,
so successful chart readers will be flexible in their approach and should
not become dogmatic. Success in looking for and capitalizing on chart
patterns will result from experience. Looking at many, many charts to
find patterns and their subsequent results is the best way to gain experience and develop confidence in identifying these formations.

Time

Location can also be thought of in respect to time. Should we be wor-
ried about a possible head-and-shoulders top pattern that is only six
months up from a major low with a cycle of four to four and a half
years? I would tend to discount or potentially look to rename that
pattern. We might consider this to be a head-and-shoulders failure if
prices rally to new highs. If we saw that same pattern develop more
than three years from the last cycle low, then we could be witnessing
something important and in the right location! We might also keep in
mind that there were at least six bull markets in the United States
that lasted for an extended period of time and produced frustrated

technicians who saw potential tops too early. The 2002–2007 market was one of those extended bull markets. Thus, the timing of the formation is important, in my opinion.

The timing of the location of the top pattern can also relate to whether we are looking at a stock from the front of the cycle or one from the back end. The financial, utility, and telecom stocks tend to be considered early leaders in bull markets or the "front end" of the market when viewed by sectors. Stocks that are sensitive to the direction of interest rates are generally viewed as the front end. As interest rates move up at the end of a business cycle, the increased cost of money tends to impact these companies first. Commodity prices or materials and energy costs tend to get bid up more in the late stages of a business cycle as raw materials become scarcer or supplies tighter. Materials, energy, and commodity plays tend to turn up late and down late in a market cycle of four to four and one half years and thus represent the "back end" of the stock market. So when we look at a mature bull market, we should be spotting top patterns in financial stocks long before energy and commodity stocks.

I haven't made an exacting study of this, but it would be my gut instinct that the time to form tops on many of the so-called penny stocks are shorter because people tend to know that the life cycles of these companies are not as long as blue-chip names. Institutional money managers tend to focus on stocks trading above $5 per share, and the fundamental coverage of stocks above $5 is where nearly all the attention is focused. I believe that the phrase "easy come, easy go" holds a lot of significance in this part of the investment arena.

The top formations that one can find in 2007 that are approximately four years up from the 2002–2003 bottom are significant in that they measure several quarters across (see **Figure 4.4**, **Figure 4.5**, and **Figure 4.6**).

The chart in Figure 4.4 shows the housing index (HGX), which nearly tripled in just two and a half years into its top in 2005.

The Financial Select Sector SPDR (XLF), represented by the exchange-trade fund (ETF) in Figure 4.5, did not triple in the 2002–2007 bull market, but it had an uninterrupted advance for more than four years.

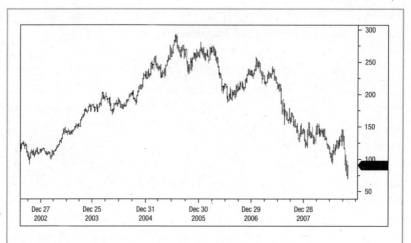

FIGURE 4.4   Housing index (HGX) tops and bottoms, 2002–2007

Source: Bloomberg

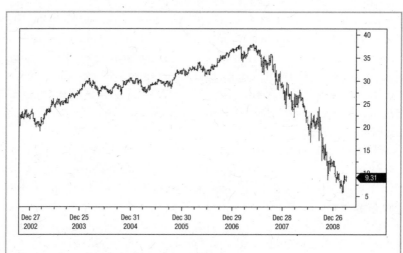

FIGURE 4.5   XLF SPDR, 2002–2008

Source: Bloomberg

FIGURE 4.6   **iShares Cohen & Steers Realty Majors (ICF),**
2002–2007

Source: Bloomberg

REITs (Real Estate Investment Trusts) soared during the 2002–2007 bull market. The ETF in Figure 4.6, the iShares Cohen & Steers Realty Majors (ICF), climbed steadily for four years and was a "triple." Early 2006 was the right time to look for a top formation.

There can and always will be exceptions, but if a pattern has the right shape but the wrong location, there is little you can do about it. There are so many listed securities we can trade that we have no compelling reason to devote time, energy, and money to patterns in the wrong location because they will not change. The best chance for success with any investment is to find those opportunities where a number of technical clues combine favorably at the same time.

Something to Reverse

Having something to reverse—by this I mean that a major top reversal needs to follow a major advance—for example, a multiyear markup from $5 to $75 per share. If you scan the charts of 2006–2007, you can find many names that had gone up four- or fivefold and had something to reverse. Declines can and do happen to stocks that have not had a major advance, but it will probably take a broad bear market to precipitate a decline. In broad bear markets, 80 to 90 percent of all stocks decline. Bear markets in equities are typically brought on by weak economic conditions, such as a recession or a credit crisis. A recession or credit crisis will have a negative effect on most companies as it hits their bottom line. A few companies—cigarette makers, utilities, and some drug firms—hold up better in a recession because these areas are often considered "recession-proof," and they are the 10 percent or so of the market that is *countercyclical*. The stock prices of recession-proof companies attract investment flows as a bear market develops.

Breaking a Key Trend Line

As top patterns unfold, they often break major up trends (see **Figure 4.7**) and longer-term moving averages, such as the 150-, 200-, or even 300-day moving average (see **Figure 4.8** and **Figure 4.9**). Prices do not actually have to start declining to break an up trend. We can break the series of higher highs and higher lows by trading sideways in a neutral trend of roughly equal lows and highs. (This will become

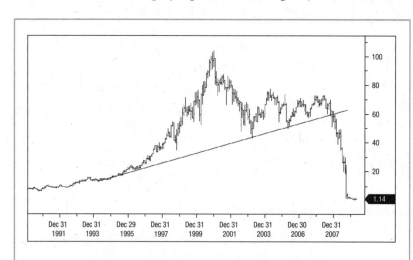

FIGURE 4.7   **AIG and its long-term up-trend line being broken**

Source: Bloomberg

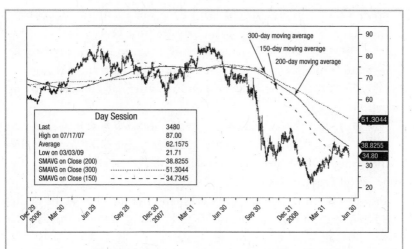

FIGURE 4.8 Caterpillar (CAT) is another member of the exclusive DJIA. In the second half of 2007, it turned down below its flat 150-, 200-, and 300-day moving averages.

Source: Bloomberg

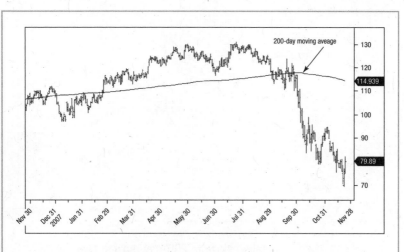

FIGURE 4.9 IBM breaks out below the 200-day moving average, an important sign of a top.

Source: Bloomberg

clearer in the following discussion of the head-and-shoulders top.) Technicians for perhaps the past forty or fifty years have been using the 200-day simple moving average as an indicator of a stock's long-term trend. In the course of a major top pattern, it is not unusual to find that a stock has broken below its flat 200-day moving average line.

In Figure 4.7, the insurance giant AIG breaks below a twelve-year up trend in late 2006. This former member of the Dow Jones Industrial Average (DJIA) broke down earlier than other Dow stocks in the 2007–2009 bear market.

Figure 4.8 shows Caterpillar (CAT), another member of the exclusive DJIA. In the second half of 2007, it turned down below its flat 150-, 200-, and 300-day moving averages.

In Figure 4.9, notice how IBM weakened steadily once it clearly broke below its 200-day moving average.

In **Figure 4.10**, Boeing Company (BA) reversed its upward course when it closed below its 200-day moving average. Notice how a later

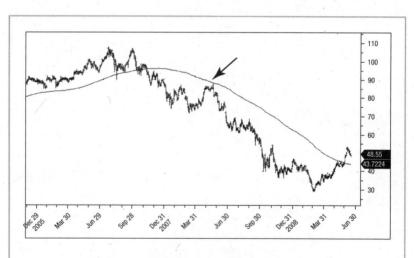

FIGURE 4.10   **Boeing breaks below its 200-day moving average and rallies back to the underside of the moving average line.**

Source: Bloomberg

rally failed at the underside of the now-declining 200-day moving average.

Volume

The volume in a major top pattern tends to reflect the idea of stock positions going from strong hands (early informed buyers and investors) to weak hands (late less-foresighted traders and the general public). The early buyers in a base pattern tend to be the early sellers in a top pattern. Just as the buyers could easily accumulate a long position from discouraged sellers, they can be early sellers to new anxious buyers just discovering this stock when valuations are rich and the story is largely discounted in the higher price levels. The best or heaviest volume within a top formation is usually during the first rally as the early investors take their profits by selling to the new enthusiastic buyers.

News About the Company and the General Economy

Stock prices generally lead the economy by six to nine months and thus the economic news and company news does not always fit the price action. The Standard & Poor's 500 Index (S&P) is included in the Conference Board Leading Economic Index (LEI). When stocks are at a low and making a bottom, the news is typically negative; only farsighted investors will buy in the face of adversity. When the price of a stock does not decline on what is perceived to be negative news, it is because the news is already discounted and reflected in the price. This can be an important tip for chart watchers. The news will be bullish at a top in the market, but farsighted investors will take their profits. When a stock does not advance on bullish news, it is because the good news is already discounted at the higher price level. This is a bearish tip that should prompt you to reexamine any long positions or anticipated purchases. During a major up trend or down trend in prices, the news and price action should be in sync.

The Classic Head-and-Shoulders Top Pattern

The head-and-shoulders top pattern is perhaps the most popular and most quoted pattern by technicians and nontechnicians.

According to Steve Nison in his book, *Japanese Candlestick Charting Techniques* (New York Institute of Finance, 1991, page 107), the Japanese candlestick pattern of the three-Buddha top is analogous to the head-and-shoulders top. The pattern copies the arrangement in Buddhist temples of a large central Buddha surrounded by smaller Buddhas or saints. The three-Buddha pattern in Japan preceded the use of the head-and-shoulders pattern in America by more than 150 years.

Technicians are serious about the head-and-shoulders pattern, although many nontechnicians often cite the pattern as "proof" of the approach being less than credible or even outright voodoo. Over the past forty years, from my investment courses as a college student to work on Wall Street and back to college as a teacher of technical analysis, I have often heard something like this: "How could you make investment decisions based on something called a 'head-and-shoulders pattern?'" I am not sure that technical analysis would be more accepted on the college campus or more acceptable even to the media if the head-and-shoulders pattern was renamed to something more serious sounding.

The head-and-shoulders pattern is really three rallies with the middle rally higher than the other two (see **Figure 4.11**). The head-and-shoulders top, when combined with volume, sentiment, news, and a bit of experience, can create an epiphany when students and professionals finally "get it." How do we find a true head-and-shoulders top? First, we have to deal with the right location. Next, the right shape.

As an example, let's consider a stock that has been building a base—literally going sideways—for months or even years. (One study of big bases in 1978 by Raymond Hanson Jr. and Robert K. Mann used at least eleven quarters as one of their prerequisites in scanning for bases in their book, *Non-Random Profits* (Freedom Press of Rhode Island, 1978.)) During the base pattern, long-term investors have been quietly accumulating the stock on weakness and hopefully getting a dividend while they wait. Let's look at an energy firm, such as Occidental Petroleum (OXY) (**Figure 4.12**), that went sideways from 1998 to 2003, even as the price of crude oil rose fivefold from

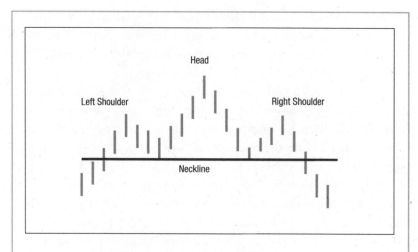

FIGURE 4.11   **Head-and-shoulders top pattern**

Source: Data courtesy of recognia (www.recognia.com).

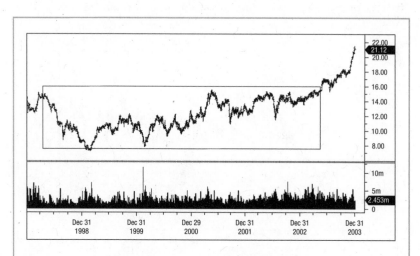

FIGURE 4.12   **Occidental Petroleum (OXY), 1998–2003**

Source: Bloomberg

$8 barrel to $40 per barrel (**Figure 4.12a**). Eventually, the stock broke out of its long base and began a dramatic bull run. Prices can sometimes go up five to ten times the price of the base, and indeed, OXY went from $20 to $120 before a two-for-one split.

After a prolonged price rise, the story on any stock under consideration can change. Now this stock is no longer cheap or undervalued. Now, after a three-to-four-year advance, many recognize the company and have bid up the price of the stock. The stock was perhaps a page sixteen story in section C of the *Wall Street Journal* in 2003, and now it is frontpage news and a feature story in *Barron's,* for example. The stock may have had little Wall Street coverage a few years earlier, and now eight or ten sell-side analysts cover it. The public is involved in the ownership of the stock, and people recognize and look forward to seeing the CEO on their business channel. All this attention creates an atmosphere of increased volume and volatility when the public comes in to buy the stock. This new volume and volatility creates the environment in which the long-term investors can quickly become scale-up profit takers without attracting attention and without depressing the stock. When a holder of stock sells out his position in pieces as prices rise, it is selling on a scale up. Confidence in the stock's

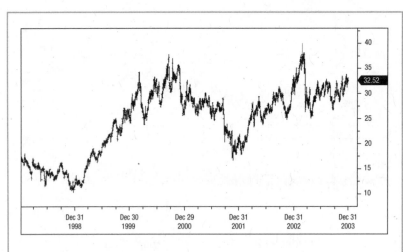

FIGURE 4.12a   **The price of crude oil 1998–2003**

Source: Bloomberg

performance is high, and the attention is a narcotic: the more investors get, the more they want. It is in the bullish environment where the left shoulder is formed.

The left shoulder is a rally to a high that at some point hits resistance, and there is enough profit-taking to stop the advance and start a correction. The volume of trading is good on the rally and light on the pullback as people are still in a bullish mood; thus, the selling is light. Prices retreat, but hold at a support area, and then after a number of weeks, there is another rally attempt that takes prices to a new all-time high or at least something above the left shoulder. The product of this rally is called the *head*. Volume does expand on this rally, but the pace of the volume should be less than what was seen on the left shoulder's advance. Similar to the left shoulder, the stock encounters profit-taking and a correction to the downside, which should end in the area of the first pullback.

With two rallies and two pullbacks, we can now draw a tentative trend line along the lows; this is commonly known as a *neckline*. In **Figure 4.13**, we can see the horizontal neckline on Deutsche Bank at just around $120, tested in March and August.

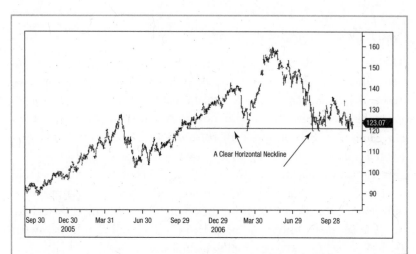

FIGURE 4.13   **Chart of Deutsche Bank AG with a head-and-shoulders top and neckline drawn along the lows.**

Source: Bloomberg

After the first two rallies—the left shoulder and head—the stock rallies once more from the neckline. Sometimes the identification of the neckline isn't clear until this third rally. This third rally does not make a new high, and the stock eventually turns down to the neckline once again. Volume does increase on this rally, but again, it is more likely to be less than the volume seen on either the rally to the head and left shoulder. Low volume on this right shoulder is pretty compelling evidence that the overall price structure has been weakened. If volume increases significantly on the right shoulder, it could mean that some other price pattern is developing.

Once prices approach the neckline, greater attention should be paid. Yet another bounce to the upside could occur, but this is when the pattern usually resolves itself to the downside. A break under the neckline is most often accompanied by a significant increase in volume. Why? At this point when prices are trading below the neckline, everyone who bought the stock (from those selling from their portfolio accumulated at the last cycle low) is now at a loss. The desire to sell has just gone up dramatically, and people have a compelling reason to dump their holdings, usually causing the volume to swell.

Head-and-Shoulders Failure

A head-and-shoulders failure happens when prices hold the neckline and then rally to new highs, as we can see in **Figure 4.14** with the price of crude oil. I once heard someone explain that this pattern was like someone rocking a car that was stuck in snow by trying a forward gear and then going into reverse. Back and forth, back and forth—and you don't know if you'll break free to the upside or downside. The authors of the older texts felt that the necklines of the true head–and–shoulder patterns should be close to horizontal, while later authors seemed to have no problems with upward- or slightly downward-sloping necklines. The early technicians also felt that a "drooping" neckline on a head-and-shoulders pattern was indicative of rapidly developing technical weakness.

What goes on during the right shoulder can be the key to a proper resolution. Is the news about the company bullish? Maybe the news is very bullish and prices don't rally to a new high. Personal experience has told me time and again that this is a turning point that shouldn't

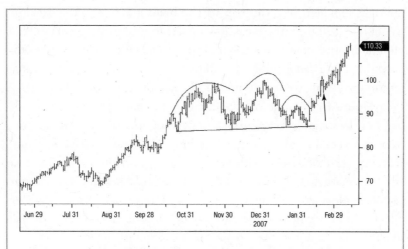

FIGURE 4.14 Head-and-shoulders failure on the price of crude
oil. Everything one looks for in a head-and-shoulders
top pattern appears to be here, but prices break
out to a new high.

Source: Bloomberg

be ignored. Even fundamentally driven investors should take notice
when a stock does not respond to seemingly bullish news. This goes
to the essence of technical analysis: markets are discounting mecha-
nisms—they are forward looking. Pure technicians might look askance
at combining news with the price action, but I see it as an advantage
you should use for your benefit. When a security ignores or doesn't
respond to bullish news, it is time to get defensive or, at the very least,
watch your positions more closely.

Targets

Price projections from the head-and-shoulders top are really straightfor-
ward and set the format for pretty much all other bar-chart price projections. It is easy and quick to measure the distance in dollars or points from
the neckline to the top of the head, or the second rally. This distance is
then projected downward from the breakdown from the neckline after

the right shoulder. So if **the top of the head** is $20 from the neckline, we subtract $20 from the breakdown point to give us an initial target or minimum price objective. I use the word *initial* because many times the downside move can extend beyond this projection. Because this is a major top formation, we should not be shocked by a major decline.

In **Figure 4.15**, Public Service Enterprise Group Incorporated (PEG) breaks down from a head-and-shoulders top formation. The distance from the neckline to the top of the head is approximately $13. Subtracting $13 from the neckline after the right shoulder would give you a $28 target ($41 − $13 = $28), which is reached and exceeded in October–November 2008.

The downside price projection can be modified by what the overall stock market is doing, any major areas of support or prior resistance, and the security's overall historic price level. A downside price objective from a large head-and-shoulders top pattern may be reached, and prices could decline further, perhaps correcting 50 percent of the prior major advance. With a head-and-shoulders top pattern, we also have to discuss what is called a *return move*.

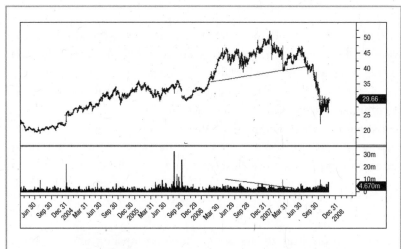

FIGURE 4.15   **PEG breaks down from a head-and-shoulders top
                formation**

Source: Bloomberg

One caveat of forecasting price targets from charts: some analysts who certainly accept the idea that charts show the results of human behavior (like greed and fear) find it hard to believe that charts can predict the precise extent of price moves. Other analysts steer away from forecasting because it can create some unforeseen risks for themselves and traders. Imagine that an analyst is quoted on CNBC or in the financial press with a target for a widely held stock or the DJIA. Once his target is "out there," his ego can get very involved. Unconsciously, analysts tend to downplay news or reports that might derail their forecast and talk up items that support their view. Traders call this "talking your book." Ideally, analysts should learn to keep an open mind and be flexible to change. This is even more important for traders who have money at stake in addition to their egos. In a way, trading is an art in which the successful adapt to what happens and manage to stay objective. A successful trader takes positions in the direction of the probabilities and adjusts quickly when wrong. Analysts who stubbornly hold to reaching a price target or who ignore a new trend can be hazardous to your wealth.

Return Moves

Return moves can be either gifts or frustrating bounces. Once a stock has broken below the neckline, it often continues lower without interruption. The return move on a head-and-shoulders top is pretty much a bounce: prices rebound back toward the bottom or underside of the neckline. Ideally, the return move should stop at or just short of the neckline, as investors who are long the stock from higher levels are now highly motivated to sell at breakeven, if possible, or to just cut their losses. The neckline acted as a support during the formation of the top, but now the role is reversed, as the people who bought against the support of the neckline turn into sellers. The role of the neckline is reversed to resistance. The return move is usually on light volume, and there is no guarantee that it even appears. In **Figure 4.16**, Public Service breaks the neckline, but quickly rallies back to the underside.

The odds of a return move developing are dependent on two circumstances. First, if the stock market has not turned into an outright bear market, as bear-market traders are more motivated sellers.

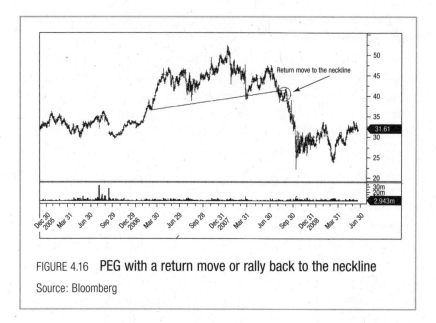

FIGURE 4.16   **PEG with a return move or rally back to the neckline**

Source: Bloomberg

Second, if the break of the neckline was not on heavy volume. Heavy volume on the break tells the chart watcher that many longs are liquidating their positions and the down trend is more likely to continue. Moderate or light volume on the break suggests that traders did not dump their positions and there could be a bounce or return move. Take advantage of the return move: sell if you didn't and short the rally if you have the disposition.

■ Tactics and Trading Strategy

Real life is not always accommodating. You can have a top failure (i.e., rally to new highs), or a breakdown that doesn't travel very far, or even two right shoulders; therefore, one should wait for a break under the neckline. Traders should sell or close out their long positions and, if inclined, go short on the break of the neckline. Other money management rules could come into play, but a buy stop for a short position should be just above the right shoulder or the last peak. A short position could also be entered if there is a return move toward the neckline. The short should be initiated only after a downside reversal or pivot below the neckline. In this instance, the buy stop should be just above the neckline.

A head-and-shoulders top works better if the stock is extended, the volume pattern is correct, and the overall market is topping or already headed down.

Variations on the Head-and-Shoulder Top

Shoulder–head–shoulder is the textbook pattern, but we can also find tops with two left shoulders, two heads instead of one, or two right shoulders. **Figure 4.17,** a chart of the iShares Technology ETF (XLK), shows a head-and-shoulders top with two right shoulders.

A number of rounded tops might be considered variations of head-and-shoulders patterns with less amplitude. There could also be variations with two heads, two left shoulders, and only one right shoulder. Remember to be flexible and open to top patterns that do not look like something out of a textbook.

Symmetry

Symmetry can give you a sense of timing. If a chart shows that six months have been spent on the left shoulder and up to the peak of

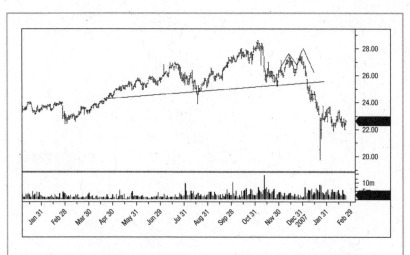

FIGURE 4.17   **A head-and-shoulders top with two right shoulders on XLK**

Source: Bloomberg

the head, then you can roughly expect that another six months will be needed for the rest of the head and the right shoulder.

In **Figure 4.18**, a chart of PEG, notice how three months are needed to develop the first half of this top pattern and another three months for the second part.

The pattern offers a sense of timing; use it to check the calendar for news or events that might be released around that time period when the pattern should be complete. This is a great heads-up that can prepare you for a possible break of the neckline. Of course, not all market-moving events can be anticipated, but being prepared for a neckline break instead of reacting to it can make a world of difference in your performance.

The Double Top

Understanding double tops should be a snap after you have mastered the head-and-shoulders top. Some analysts have called the double top an "M" formation because it looks like the thirteenth letter of the

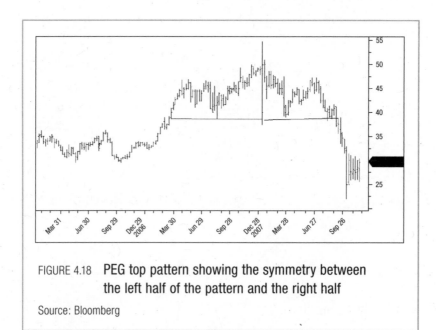

FIGURE 4.18   **PEG top pattern showing the symmetry between the left half of the pattern and the right half**

Source: Bloomberg

alphabet. Over the years, I have found that double tops are a fairly reliable pattern, especially in the fixed-income market, although other analysts have considered true double tops to be rare events. The double top is a rally in a stock to a level at which there is sufficient supply of stock to satisfy all the buyers and generate a downward reaction. Traders and investors will have various reasons to sell, but in general, the marketplace will feel that the stock has gone as high as it is likely to go for the moment. Some of the older technical books suggest that the reaction from the first top should be greater than 5 percent; others suggest that a 20-percent reaction from the first peak is needed for a true double top. After the 5-percent to 20-percent reaction, prices rally again to a second peak. The time elapsed before the second peak is reached should be more than a month, or it is likely to be part of some other pattern. When weighing the factors that go into a double top, the time between the peaks has been a larger issue in the old texts than the amount of the retracement from the first peak.

Figure 4.19 shows a clear double-top pattern on Starbucks (SBUX). Though the pattern is called a *double top,* the two peaks do not have to form at the exact same price level, and they do not have to be so exact.

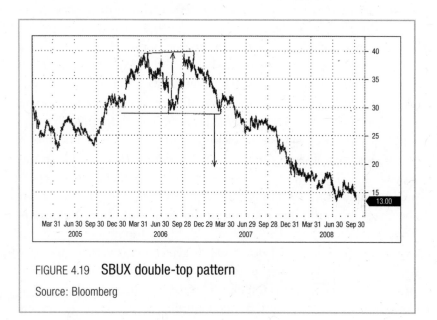

FIGURE 4.19   **SBUX double-top pattern**

Source: Bloomberg

Over my years of chart reading, I have developed a rule of thumb that the second peak can be 1 percent or 2 percent *below* or *above* the first peak. The reasoning behind this is fairly simple: traders who did not sell out on the first peak, who have learned not to hold out for the last penny, or who have become more anxious sellers will look to sell at 98, 98.50, 99, and 99.50—just below the first peak of 100. The reason why prices can also go 1 percent or 2 percent above the first peak is due to the market electing the protective buy stops entered by traders shorting the security. Prices might rally just enough to hit those buy stops before turning down in earnest. If the second peak goes more than 2 percent higher than the first high, it is no longer considered a double top.

Another qualifier is that the distance or time between peaks should be at least one month so that the peaks are not part of the same consolidation formation. The psychology of the traders and investors might play out like this: after the reaction or sell-off from the first peak, some of the weaker holders of the stock may decide they missed a great opportunity to sell and are looking to take profits in the area of the first peak. The reaction down from the first peak can also bring in bargain hunters and others who go long on the stock and are looking to take profits in the area of the first peak. As prices approach the second peak, long-term investors sell the remaining stock they accumulated earlier, weak holders who didn't sell earlier are now sellers, and the supply of stock is enough to turn prices back down again. If or when prices drop below the recent low, it will be clear that the supply of stock is greater than the demand, and the path will trend downward. Volume tends to increase around each of the peaks, but trading can be heavy on one peak and light on the other or even light on both peaks and still show a potent top formation. If most of the conditions of a double top are not seen or met, then the trader should be on guard and suspicious. The downside price objective from the double top is generated by taking the distance in points or dollars from the low between the two peaks to a line connecting the two highs. This distance is projected down from the neckline (Starbucks top at $40, as seen in Figure 4.19). The initial downside target can be overrun, but this isn't a problem. The initial projection can be doubled for a secondary or lower target, or you can look backward in time to the left part of the chart to see where support might develop. Symmetry is good with a double top, and the distance from the first top can be projected from the peak to anticipate the second peak. While there are no complex double tops like the head-and-shoulders variations, sometimes a platform or shelf might form after the second peak. A double top with a platform is the only nontextbook pattern and is rarer than the double bottom with a platform (see Chapter 5). The double top is what it is. In 2009, some analysts saw a very large double top in the S&P 500, which projected down to approximately 150! (See **Figure 4.20.**) When the double-top pattern was "discovered" in the early part of the 1900s, the chartists did not have that much data to work with, and I don't believe that they would consider this a valid example of a double top. We gain confidence in chart patterns when we see them play out to completion, and this possible top could take many more years to play out.

Targets

The target for the double top is derived by taking the distance from the reaction low between the two peaks to the top of the pattern. The best way to identify the top of the pattern is to draw a line across the

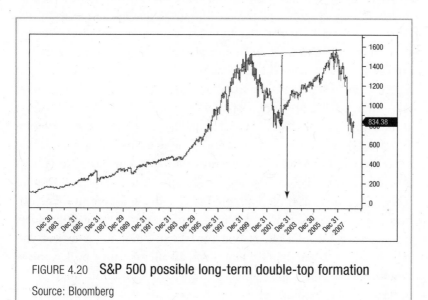

FIGURE 4.20   **S&P 500 possible long-term double-top formation**

Source: Bloomberg

top peaks. This distance is then projected downward from the reaction low between the two peaks.

■ Tactics and Trading Strategy

When trading the double top, longs should be sold. Shorts could be considered when prices break below the neckline or support level between the two rally peaks. The buy stop should go above the top of the higher of the two peaks. In practice, this might be too much risk relative to the potential reward, and a buy stop just above the midpoint between the neckline and the top of the second peak might be a more appropriate level of risk. The reason for this particular risk point is that if prices can rally back more than 50 percent of this decline, then they are in "bullish territory" and the bears are on the defensive.

The Triple Top

Once you have seen a double top, it is not hard to understand a *triple top.* A triple-top pattern shows three roughly equal peaks in an advance or up trend. The triple top is simple but is relatively rarely seen in practice. There are three rally attempts resembling a head–and–shoulders top, but these are three roughly equal highs. I used to think triple tops were rare, but in the 2008 bear market I found several triple tops that preceded some big declines. There is one significant risk with a triple top in that the top can become a consolidation pattern, like a rectangle, and we might see a bullish breakout. A triple top is not a double top with just one more rally attempt. The three peaks of a triple top are not spaced as far apart as the two peaks of a double top. The pullbacks or corrections between the peaks do not have to hold at the same level. In addition, the three peaks are not expected to be precisely the same, but our 1-percent to 2-percent rule used for double tops can be applied here. Some analysts are more generous with triple tops and indicate that a 3-percent difference between peak levels can be accepted. Similar to a head-and-shoulders top pattern, volume should decline from the first peak to the second, and then the third. When the neckline is broken after the third peak, volume should expand significantly to give credibility to the confirmation of the pattern. Getting an initial price objective from the triple top is no different from the head-and-shoulders pattern or double top—the height from the neckline to any of the peaks is projected downward from the neckline. This method of deriving an objective is no different from a double top, but our instincts would say that there is more distribution from a triple top than a double top, and a lower price target should result. Triple tops are sometimes referred to as "W" patterns because of the three points.

Targets

A price target from a triple top is derived from the height of the pattern from the neckline to top of the pattern. This height or distance is projected downward from the neckline to give us our potential price target. See how the target is nearly reached on American Oil & Gas (AEZ) in **Figure 4.21**.

■ Tactics and Trading Strategy

Traders need to close out or sell long positions, or go short on a break below the support level at the low of the troughs between the three

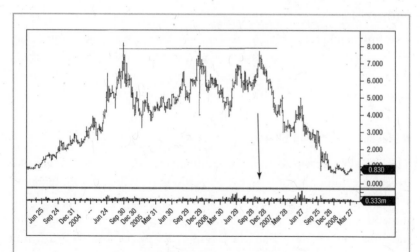

FIGURE 4.21   **A large triple-top formation on AEZ with the downside price projection**

Source: Bloomberg

peaks, with a buy stop just above the highest high of the pattern. A
short position could be timed using a pivot point or other reversal signal
if prices rally to the support level that was broken.

The Broadening Top

Technicians in the 1920s seemed to find a number of broadening tops
in 1929, but their frequency has declined over the years. Personally, I
have found the broadening formation to be rare and can sometimes be
a continuation pattern instead of a top reversal. The classic broadening
top has three higher peaks or rallies, and between them, two lower bottoms with the second bottom lower than the first. The pattern looks like
the bell of the trumpet or trombone. The reversal points of the pattern
should not be too spread out, not more than two months apart. If the
swings were spread far apart, the seemingly wild swings up and down
would probably not seem so wild, and the high volume would probably
drift away to some other security that was making a new high.

Targets

The broadening top formation does not have a real price target that
is measured like the other top patterns in this chapter. Basically, when
the last peak is reached and prices start down in earnest, they will break
below the lowest point of the broadening formation.

■ Tactics and Trading Strategy

The broadening top formation is difficult to identify, with high and
irregular volume throughout the formation and wild and unintelligent
swings. The trader is going long at the new high and going short or just
stopped out at the new low. We want to sell or short the breakout on
the broadening pattern, but where is it? Once prices are well below the
last low point, we can truly see the pattern, but this means we are well
off the top. Since we are near an important top and likely at the end
of an up trend, we can get an advance warning. This advance warning
is the last rally; if it doesn't break above the preceding rally, then it is a
harbinger of the coming decline.

The Inverted-V Top

The *spike top,* or *inverted-V top,* is very dynamic and powerful, but among the toughest to analyze or anticipate. With the other major top patterns covered—head and shoulders, double top, and triple top—a battle between bulls and bears takes place over a long period of time. This interplay between buyers and sellers sets up or prepares the market for the next move. The spike top or inverted-V formation has no progression from up trend to sideways and then down trend; instead there is a sharp reversal with little foreshadowing (see **Figure 4.22**).

The inverted-V top formation has three parts. First, there is a fairly sharp and extensive advance. The second part will be a high-volume pivot marking the top. This climax session could be described as a *key reversal* or a *two-day reversal.* Sometimes, volume on the turn may be light, which could be thought of as a market that had run of out steam. After this pivot, prices turn down and break the up trend. Some technicians have noticed a symmetry between the up trend and the down trend with respect to similar angles of ascent and descent that seem to approximate a 45-degree angle.

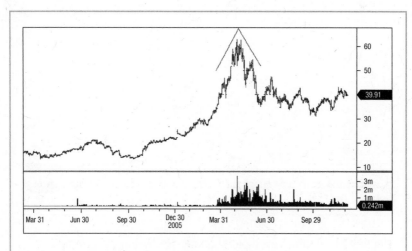

FIGURE 4.22   **An inverted V-top on Andersons Inc.**

Source: Bloomberg

Targets

The inverted-V top does not have a formal price target. With this pattern, one should expect a significant decline on the order of 50 percent or more of the prior advance. In **Figure 4.23**, the entire rally before the V top is wiped out.

■ Tactics and Trading Strategy

Longs should be sold or liquidated when you identify the pivot top or if an up trend is broken after the top. Traders who find they are confronting an inverted-V top should be careful and alert for false signals.

The Saucer Top

The *saucer*, or *rounded*, top is similar to a head-and-shoulders top, but with little amplitude and the rallies flattened out. Other analysts have described the saucer as a line formation with some amplitude, while others call the saucer a cup or bowl. Prices rally until they slowly meet resistance and gradually curve downward. Looking for symmetry in the pattern, or perhaps, news items when prices are poised to break down

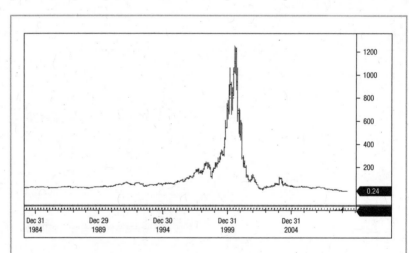

FIGURE 4.23   **Another example of an inverted V-top with Nortel Networks**

Source: Bloomberg

holds little promise: company announcements often come later after the stock has broken down. Volume tends to follow the path of prices, expanding as prices creep higher and diminishing as prices retreat. The saucer pattern (and the line pattern) lacks height, and thus creates a small problem in coming up with reasonable price targets. This can be remedied by looking back on the chart for a major resistance area, which would be expected to act as major support on the decline. One could also do some quick math and figure out a one-third to two-thirds retracement of the rally prior to the top, or one could consult a point-and-figure chart for a downside "count" or price projection. Rounded tops are generally less common than rounded bottoms and can be seen on weekly or monthly charts.

Targets

The rounded top or saucer top is a gradual change in the supply and demand for a security that slowly picks up momentum on the downside, reversing the prior up trend. It is difficult to find a clear breakout point and a conventional price target, but these tops are usually followed by meaningful declines. A good example of a rounded top can be seen in **Figure 4.24**.

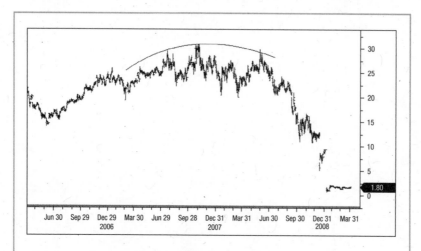

FIGURE 4.24 **A rounded or saucer top on Satyam Computer Services, Ltd.**

Source: Bloomberg

■ Tactics and Trading Strategy

Traders have a lot of time to take positions when they find a saucer top. They can sell longs or probe the short side when prices have stopped rising and have begun to level off or have turned down. Shorts could also be considered if there is a clear point where prices could be seen breaking lower.

CHAPTER 5

Major Bottoms

A MASTERY OF MAJOR BOTTOM patterns should proceed in three steps. First, understand how different traders and investors behave during a bottom. Second, learn how to identify bottoms. Third, add identifying bottoms to your investment-skills toolbox with the proper tactics. Few people are comfortable with following just one investment approach. There are many successful money managers who often blend fundamentals with some technicals, such as the 200-day simple moving average or the relative strength of the stock, industry, or sector versus the Standard & Poor's (S&P) 500 Index. Also, many practical technicians actually do listen to the fundamentals because the two approaches should be in agreement during major up trends and down trends. Using any of a number of different charting approaches (for example, line charts, bar charts, candlesticks, or point-and-figure charts), a bottom pattern shows a stock or other security that has been trading sideways and is about to begin a rally. A major bottom pattern should be found following a declining trend of significance (unless it's an initial public offering, and thus has little price history to work with), suggesting that a turnaround to the upside lies ahead.

Investors Make Bottoms

During a bottom, the fundamentals are probably bearish and match the tape or price action. As a bottom unfolds over a number of quarters, the fundamentals may well show some subtle improvement. If you read the daily business papers, or even just the business section of a major metropolitan paper, you should be able to notice when prices stop reacting downward to bearish news.

Years ago at a seminar in Las Vegas, I learned from one of the speakers and a longtime friend in the business, Richard Edwards, that the word *despite* was the most powerful word in technical analysis. Financial journalists will look to explain today's price action in the marketplace with today's news reports. Journalists are trained in school or on the job to construct a news story with an attention-grabbing eighty-character headline. The first paragraph or the lead "graph" comes next with all the "news" of the day. Nearly all the so-called news of the day is about the past—last month's sales figures, last quarter's earnings, or last week's unemployment claims or inventory figures. Most traders and investors anticipate the news instead of reacting to it. We look at the trend of unemployment claims and project the next week. We look at the pace of earnings and revenues and estimate the current quarter. The old Wall Street saying, "buy the rumor and sell the news," goes to the essence of investors anticipating the news. As traders and investors buy and sell in anticipation of some release, they discount the news. Prices will often decline in front of bearish news and rally ahead of bullish news. However, when prices rally on the announcement of what is generally perceived as bearish news, the reporter might use a headline that includes the word *despite:* "XYZ advances despite a disappointing earnings report."

The quarterly earnings numbers were down from the prior quarter or year, and the stock should have declined but it didn't. Traders sold the stock down, anticipating the decline, and covered their shorts or went long on the announcement. Financial journalists are not taught that the markets anticipate and discount the fundamentals, so when they are unable to explain a rally developing from what seems to be bearish news, they resort to using the word *despite*. This is not an indictment of *all* reporters; some savvy journalists have found out how technical analysis works and do understand why markets are forward-looking.

Forward-looking investors are ones who will buy in the late stages of a bear market, as they are looking ahead one or two quarters or more to a turnaround in the fundamentals. Traders will continue to short or stand aside as the bottom forms because they are largely motivated by the trend. Obviously, the shorts will largely become losses.

The mentality behind major bottoms is fear. In my opinion, this very human emotion is perhaps harder to shake off and put aside than greed. Traders and sell-side analysts are generally not in a rush to pick tops. People want to believe that the good times will continue and that the stock they buy will continue to go up after they go long. Picking a top or being a bear is like being the boy who cried wolf: you are not popular on Wall Street or at cocktail parties, even if you are proven right. Bottom picking is a more accepted activity. Declaring that some asset is dirt cheap, buying it, and seeing it go still lower is easier to explain than being the one throwing water on the bull market. The public is not really involved in the bottom process, but some members are active players in a top when they have built up the confidence to finally buy. Telling people that the party is about to end when they have just arrived is not popular with investors and within sell-side research departments. But just learning to recognize a few common bottom patterns like a double bottom or a head-and-shoulders formation will put you well ahead of the pack.

Bottoms on charts display the interplay of buyers and sellers and show the move from a bear market to a new bull move, as the stock stops declining, goes sideways, and then begins a new up trend. The best bottom patterns will take many months or even years to form—something that should be easy to understand after our discussion of major tops. A large multinational company may need several quarters to alter its current deteriorating business direction, bring on a new product, or merge an acquisition and see it translate to the bottom line. Although it seems like many of today's volatile markets can just turn on a dime, sustained bull moves lasting a few years or longer are most often built on strong bottom formations that take several years to develop (see **Figure 5.1**). The base formation on Occidental Petroleum took approximately twenty years. This mirrors the twenty years of sideways price action in crude oil.

A bottom to the current bear market that started in October 2007 could develop in the fourth quarter of 2009, in my opinion, so it could prove to be a real-time exercise, watching for bottom formations while the economic news is probably still bearish. Whenever

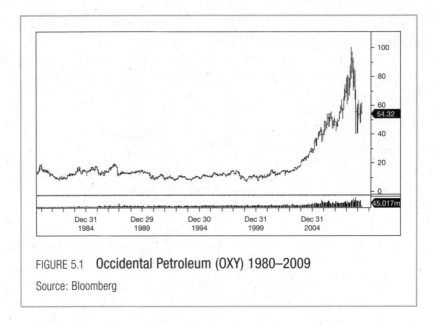

FIGURE 5.1   Occidental Petroleum (OXY) 1980–2009

Source: Bloomberg

you read (or even reread) this book, one key to spotting bottoms will be to notice when the price action is bullish while the news is still negative.

The Head-and-Shoulders Bottom

A *head-and-shoulders bottom* or, as it is also called, an *inverse head-and-shoulders pattern,* simply portrays three successive declines and rallies, with the second decline reaching a lower point than either of the other two sell-offs. The head-and-shoulders bottom is a mirror image of the head-and-shoulders top discussed in Chapter 4, *but* the volume pattern is different.

Important and valid bottoms, such as the head-and-shoulders pattern, need a down trend to be underway for some time, with prices eventually reaching a nadir in their slide, and then followed by a rally. The volume of shares traded should expand or even be heavy on the decline, then tapering off noticeably on the rally. The rally stalls, and eventually another decline follows, which takes prices below the first low or the left shoulder (see **Figure 5.2**).

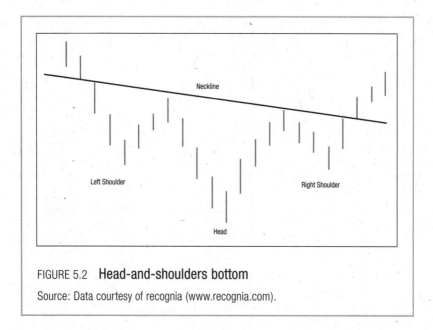

FIGURE 5.2 **Head-and-shoulders bottom**

Source: Data courtesy of recognia (www.recognia.com).

Volume increases on the second decline relative to the prior rally, but it generally is less than the volume on the first decline within the left shoulder. On the second rally, the volume should pick up again and the overall volume on the head is slightly more than during the left shoulder. There is yet a third decline that does not reach the nadir of the second low or head, and another rally ensues. Volume is really subpar on this third decline and heavy on the last rally, and it should remain heavy as the security breaks through the neckline. The neckline is drawn across the peaks of the first two rallies. The neckline might be horizontal, or it could slant downward or upward. In **Figure 5.3**, Petroleo Brazil suffers a major decline in 2008 but traces out a head-and-shoulders bottom in late 2008 that proves to be a "triple" by June 2009. This is a good example of the importance of learning to recognize a major bottom pattern. In **Figure 5.4**, Boeing makes a clear head-and-shoulders bottom in late 2002 and early 2003. Notice how volume expands.

The distance from the bottom of the second decline, or head, to the neckline connecting the rally highs is used to project an initial upside price objective or target. This distance—expressed in points,

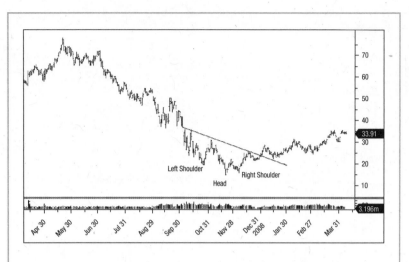

FIGURE 5.3   **Notice the downward sloped neckline on Petroleo Brazil.**

Source: Bloomberg

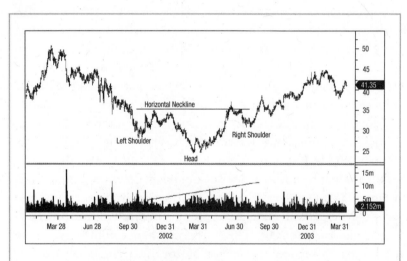

FIGURE 5.4   **The chart of Boeing in 2002–2003 shows a clear horizontal neckline on a head-and-shoulders bottom formation.**

Source: Bloomberg

thirty-seconds, or dollars and cents—is added to the breakout price level at the neckline to yield a price target.

Return Move

Similar to the head-and-shoulders top pattern discussed in Chapter 4, sometimes a return move occurs back to the neckline before the advance begins in earnest. Similar to a top, the probability of a return will be dependent on a number of "if" factors. If the breakout from the neckline was not accompanied by strong volume, there might be a pullback or return move. If this stock broke out before a broad bull market was underway, we might see a quick retreat after the breakout. You can think of it this way: this stock was ready to go up, but the background scene was not ready with a broad bull market, so we see a hesitation or return move. Some technicians believe that return moves happen more often with bottoms than tops. If you missed the breakout and were trying to buy the stock but wanted to avoid paying too much, then the return move can be your golden opportunity.

Symmetry

In Chapter 4, we discussed how the symmetry of top patterns could give you an edge in timing versus your competition, which might be ignoring chart patterns. The same is true with bottoms. If a chart shows that thirteen or sixteen weeks has been spent on the left shoulder to the bottom of the head, then we can make a crude projection that approximately another thirteen or sixteen weeks will be needed to see the rest of the head and the right shoulder play out. Like top patterns, we can check the calendar for any scheduled report or events that might be released near that time period. The prepared trader who is using the bottom pattern can time the purchase of additional stock positions near the breakout. Timing is very important to option traders who deal in a wasting asset, and one could buy relatively inexpensive calls *before* volatility has increased after the advance in prices, once the breakout through the neckline has occurred.

Targets

The distance from the bottom of the second decline, or head, to the neck–line connecting the rally highs is used to project an initial upside price objective or target. This distance—expressed in points, thirty-seconds, or dollars and cents—is added to breakout price level at the neckline to give us a price target. (See **Figure 5.5.**) In the chart of Boeing, we show the distance from the head to the neckline projected upward.

■ Tactics and Trading Strategy

Of course, you could build a long position as the formation develops, especially during the right shoulder, when you can use the low of the head as your risk point. The right shoulder could be repeated with another right shoulder (see the next section on complex head–and–shoulders pat–terns), so buying during the right shoulder could at times be premature. Traders looking to maximize their returns versus their time involvement could buy on the breakout or near the breakout from the neckline.

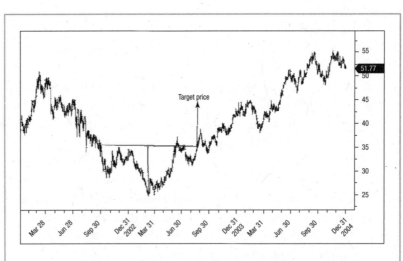

FIGURE 5.5   With Boeing again used as an example, we can see how to measure from the bottom of the head to the neckline to give us a price target from this bottom formation.

Source: Bloomberg

If there is a return move, they can buy the correction back to the neckline or add to positions on the retracement. If you are unable to buy at these spots, then you could look to buy the first short-term consolidation pattern (see Chapters 7 and 8)—for example, a flag or a pennant.

Complex Head-and-Shoulders Bottoms

Just as we saw some complex head–and–shoulders tops in Chapter 4, we can anticipate that we will eventually find a complex head–and–shoulders bottom pattern. We might find a bottom with two left shoulders, one head, and two right shoulders. See **Figure 5.6**.

Targets

Targets for a complex bottom are the same as a "classic" formation: we measure the distance from the bottom of the head to the neckline and project that distance from the breakout above the neckline. Any "extra" shoulders will not affect the target.

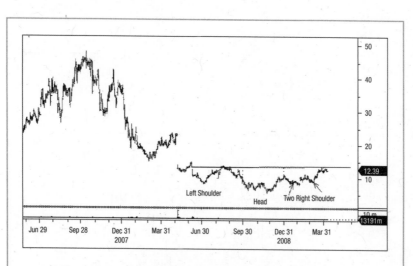

FIGURE 5.6 **A complex head-and-shoulders bottom with two right shoulders on Synchronoss Technologies**

Source: Bloomberg

■ Tactics and Trading Strategy

Both the simple, ordinary head–and–shoulders bottom and the complex bottom, if you should encounter it, should have the same approach, which would be to cover short positions or go long on the break of the neckline (or both), with a sell stop just below the last trough, whether or not there was more than one right shoulder. The sell stop is to limit losses on longs. Longs could also be established on a reversal up from the neckline if there is a return move, and the sell stop can be just below the neckline.

The Double Bottom

A *double bottom* formation has just two declines and two rallies, with the chart looking like a "W" pattern as in **Figure 5.7.** Analysts in the late 1920s and early 1930s considered the double bottom the pattern best known to the public at that time. In practice, we usually find double bottoms *after* the stock has moved up substantially from the second bottom. The reason this happens is because a stock typically will find buying interest, or what technicians call *support at a previous low.* The support at the prior low may hold

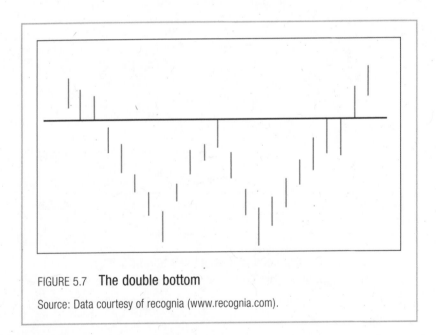

FIGURE 5.7   **The double bottom**

Source: Data courtesy of recognia (www.recognia.com).

for awhile, and then the selling overcomes the support and the decline resumes. In practice, I draw the line when the second low exceeds the first low by 2 percent. Thus, a true double bottom is identified after prices have rallied substantially from the second low.

To complicate things, volume patterns on double bottoms show a lot of variation: volume might be heavy on one low and light on the other, or light throughout. In my opinion, volume should be heavier on the second bottom because traders can buy against the support level of the first low and place a protective sell stop below the first low (see the following "Tactics and Trading Strategy" section). If you know where your stop point or risk is, you should be able to buy more aggressively, and volume should be heavier.

The double bottom can have a variation of a ledge or a platform after the rally from the second bottom or, as one technician likes to call it, a *handle* (see "The Saucer Bottom" following and **Figure 5.8**). This sideways pause after the upside breakout gives the trader another opportunity to position the security from the long side and to add to existing positions.

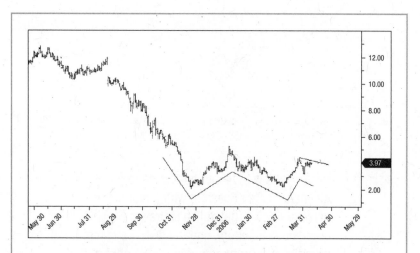

FIGURE 5.8   **This chart of JDS Uniphase shows a double-bottom pattern with about a two-week handle in March.**

Source: Bloomberg

Targets

To derive the price target from a double bottom, take the distance from an imaginary line drawn between the two lows and a horizontal line at the peak between the lows (see **Figure 5.9**). This distance in dollars or points is then projected up from the breakout point when the rally from the second low exceeds the peak between the bottoms.

Timing and Symmetry

Timing and symmetry are pretty easy to understand with a double bottom, as even just a casual look at the pattern gives the impression that there is balance and equity between the two bottoms. By measuring the distance across to the peak and shifting that to the right on your chart

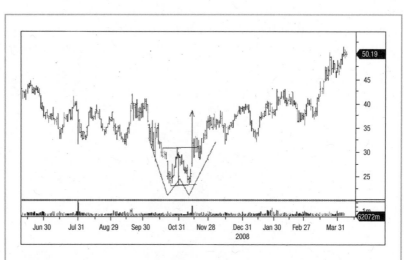

FIGURE 5.9   Here we show a double-bottom pattern on Green Mountain Coffee Roasters with the proper way to derive a price target. A line is drawn along the lows of the double bottom, and the distance is measured from this line to the top of the rally between the two lows. This distance is projected upward from the breakout point at the neckline.

Source: Bloomberg

paper or your computer screen from the first bottom or low, you can get an approximate date for when the second bottom could develop. With an early warning of when the bottom could develop, the job of the technician or trader becomes a little easier. Knowing "when" can allow you to focus more on the execution of your buys.

■ Tactics and Trading Strategy

If you see the second low in real time and prices go more than 2 percent below the level of the first bottom, then you should bail out or liquidate the position. If you were short before the pattern completes, you should cover your shorts; you could go long on the break above the resistance level at the peak between the two bottoms. If a long position is initiated, then a sell stop can be entered below the lowest low of the two troughs. An initial long or an additional long position can be established on the break of the resistance at the neckline, with a sell stop just below the broken resistance level. See **Figures 5.10** and **5.11.**

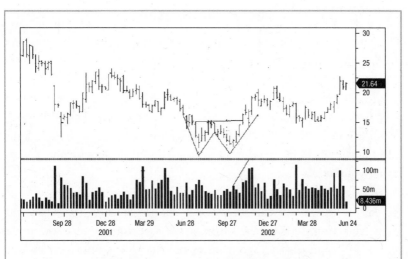

FIGURE 5.10   **Weekly chart of Hewlett-Packard. Double bottoms can be seen on intraday, daily, weekly, and monthly charts.**

Source: Bloomberg

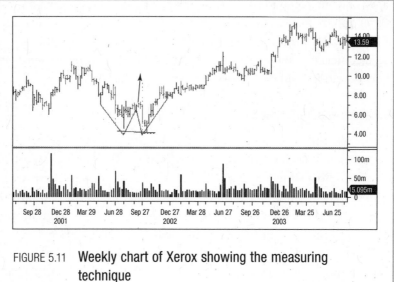

FIGURE 5.11   **Weekly chart of Xerox showing the measuring technique**

Source: Bloomberg

The Triple Bottom

The *triple bottom* could be considered a variation of a double bottom. Instead of breaking out over the peak of the rally from the first low or bottom, prices retreat again and decline to retest the lows to make a third bottom as in **Figures 5.12, 5.12a, 5.12b,** and **5.12c.** Volume is light on the first low and heavier on the second and third lows. A neckline can be drawn along the tops of the rallies, and the breakout through the neckline after the third low should be accompanied with strong volume.

To give yourself an edge in spotting a valid bottom pattern, one of the easiest things you can do is watch the interplay of the news and the price action. During the latter part of a bottom or base, the price action will typically diverge from or not match the business news or releases from the company. When stock prices are weak, the news about the company is most likely going to be negative or bearish.

Try to visualize a day on which the news initially is bearish but the stock goes up. The neophyte investor wouldn't understand why,

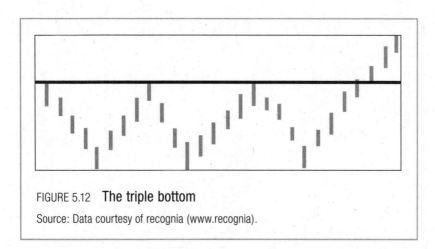

FIGURE 5.12 **The triple bottom**

Source: Data courtesy of recognia (www.recognia).

and most likely, wouldn't buy the stock; traders are most comfortable buying stocks when the news is bullish. However, a stock that doesn't go down when the news is negative tells you the bad news is already in the marketplace and prices are likely to appreciate because of buying from long-term investors who look ahead one or two or more quarters.

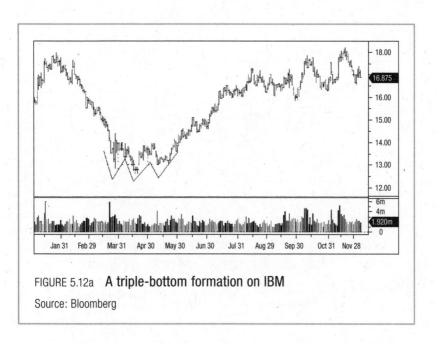

FIGURE 5.12a **A triple-bottom formation on IBM**

Source: Bloomberg

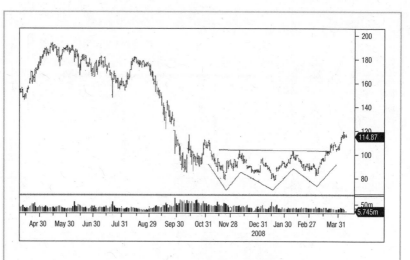

FIGURE 5.12b   **A triple-bottom formation on Apple Inc.**

Source: Bloomberg

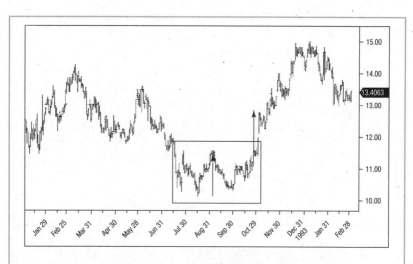

FIGURE 5.12c   **A triple-bottom formation on IBM showing how a price target is measured and projected upward**

Source: Bloomberg

Targets

To derive the price target from a triple bottom, we use the same approach that we did with the double bottom in that we take the distance from an imaginary line drawn across the lows and a horizontal line at the peaks. This distance in dollars or points is then projected up from the breakout point. See **Figure 5.12c**.

■ Tactics and Trading Strategy

The triple bottom should be traded with the closing of short trades or going long on the break above the resistance level at the high of the peaks between the three troughs, with a sell stop just below the lowest nadir. A long can be established when prices break the resistance level at the top of the peaks, with a sell stop just below the broken resistance level.

The Saucer Bottom

In Chapter 4, we looked at a rounded or saucer top. The *rounded bottom,* or *saucer bottom,* seems to be more common than the top varieties, but I haven't seen an explanation for this fact in the literature. In the 1940s and 1950s, this pattern was also called a *bowl* and the top an *inverted bowl.* In the late 1980s, William O'Neil, founder of *Investor's Business Daily* [William O'Neil, *How to Make Money in Stocks,* McGraw-Hill, 1988], introduced the *cup-with-handle pattern,* which is basically a saucer bottom with another consolidation before the breakout. Prices slowly decline in the saucer like a slow scallop, with volume slowly diminishing to a low at the bottom of the formation. Volume gradually increases as prices scallop upward in the right side of the saucer. In other words, both the volume of trading and prices show a saucer formation. Sometimes the saucer bottom has a platform or shelf before the upside breakout. This platform is different than the handle, which is usually shown with a downward slant and forms in the upper half of the saucer. Volume can become heavy at the start of the platform, and also at the end, when the security breaks out from the platform. See **Figures 5.13** and **5.13a**.

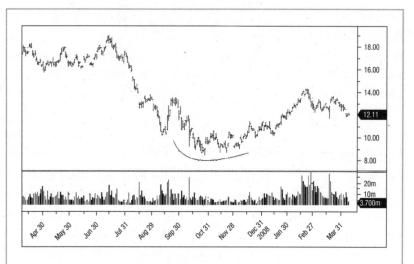

FIGURE 5.13   The saucer-bottom pattern can be seen on this
chart of SLV, the silver exchange-traded fund.

Source: Bloomberg

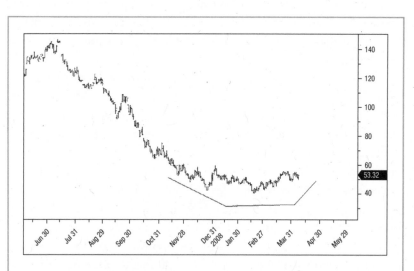

FIGURE 5.13a   A saucer bottom is developing on this chart of
crude oil futures.

Source: Bloomberg

Targets

When we covered the rounded top in Chapter 4, we noted that this pattern does not have a clear price target because this pattern is a gradual change in the supply and demand for the instrument. From the bottom, the demand slowly picks up positive momentum, reversing the previous down trend. An obvious breakout point is hard to identify, and the formation does not have much amplitude to measure, but this bottom is often followed by a significant rise. In various publications, William O'Neil suggests holding stocks that break out from a cup-and-handle pattern for a 20-percent advance in the subsequent eight weeks.

■ Tactics and Trading Strategy

Traders have plenty of time to initiate a long position as a saucer forms. There are four opportune times during the saucer formation to buy. The first time is during the upwardly curving part of the saucer when prices and volume are gradually rising. A second opportunity is at the end of the curve when the stock or security levels off on reduced volume. The formation of the platform is a third opportunity to go long, and the last opportunity is on the breakout from the platform.

The V Bottom

A *spike,* or *V bottom,* is a nerve-wracking pattern. In most of the other reversal bottoms, there is a progressive movement from down trend to base to up trend, but with the V bottom, there is no shift. The V-bottom pattern starts with a down trend, which often is fairly sharp and can be extensive. The news about this stock or commodity is probably negative and well covered in the press. Prices decline and decline until a pivot point is reached. This pivotal low can be a one-day key reversal or a two-day reversal (more on reversals in Chapter 11). Prices don't stay in this area for more than a few days. Volume will increase significantly and can be the heaviest if there is a selling climax day. A selling climax will have heavy volume and mark the end of the down trend. This climax might only be seen in retrospect unless one is closely following this security on a daily basis. See **Figures 5.14** and **5.15**.

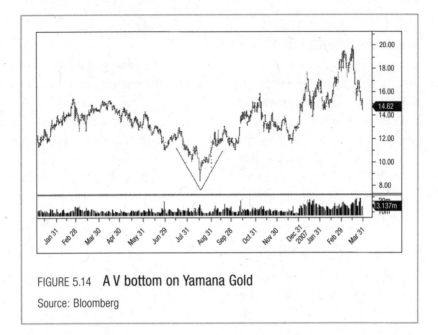

FIGURE 5.14 **A V bottom on Yamana Gold**

Source: Bloomberg

Targets

Like our mirror image as a top formation, the V bottom does not have a readable price target, but past experience tells us to anticipate a substantial move.

■ Tactics and Trading Strategy

The investor or trader should watch and wait for the V pattern to be completed, because even experienced traders have trouble with this formation. With a double bottom, we can measure the height of the pattern to give us a target, but the V does not offer us that clue. Prices will snap back on the V, but how far they travel will take some educated estimates and examination of past swings, if possible.

Summary

So now we can spot a bottom. However, we can read and study chart patterns but still fail to translate what we find into results. To convert bottoms into profits, we need to be able to see the whole picture and

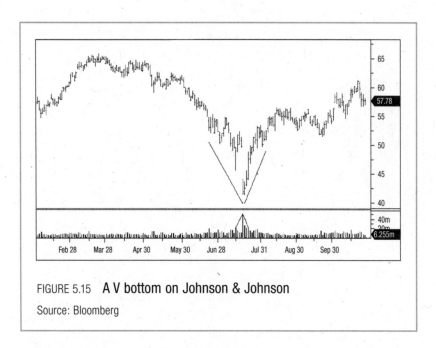

FIGURE 5.15   **A V bottom on Johnson & Johnson**

Source: Bloomberg

not hold on to an idealized pattern or wait for a textbook picture. Once you can spot a bottom formation, review the tactics, and then act on the opportunity! Confidence will increase with experience, and profits should follow. In the next several chapters, we delve into other patterns, such as triangles, wedges, and flags. These can help us navigate and profit from the down trends after major tops and the up trends that follow major bottoms.

CHAPTER 6

Triangles, Boxes, and Rectangles

TRIANGLES AND *COILS* are viewed as continuation patterns and sometimes reversal patterns, but typically not as bases and top reversals. The major top and bottom patterns that were discussed in Chapters 4 and 5 took many months, quarters, and sometimes years to unfold. Triangles should play out over several weeks or several months. Triangles and coils should be regarded as pauses in the longer-term trend of prices, and prices should continue the previous or prevailing trend before the pattern appeared. This is why triangles are considered *continuation patterns*. The continuation of the prior trend happens more often than not, but false moves happen and thus triangles do not rank among the most reliable of patterns.

In the 1920s and 1930s, *triangles* and *coils* were considered one of the most important chart patterns. R. W. Schabacker (*Stock Market Theory and Practice*, B.C. Forbes Publishing Company, 1930, page 604) thought that the swings in triangle formations were the best proof that the pool operators were involved in accumulation (bottoms) and distribution (tops). Pool operators had concentrations of capital from wealthy individuals, not unlike the hedge funds of today or the commodity pool operators in the 1970s and 1980s. Pools were in their heyday in the late 1920s in the United States. They often had written agreements among a group of investors who delegated trading authority to one manager to trade a specific stock for a specified time, and then to divide the profits or losses.

Coils resemble an isosceles triangle with the two sides of equal length and the same angle. Coils often extend out toward the apex of the pattern, but triangles typically break out approximately two-thirds to three-quarters of the way through their patterns. **Figure 6.1** shows an equilateral triangle, and **Figure 6.2** shows a coil.

When you look at a coil with its balanced sideways price action, you can see the equilibrium between the bulls and bears. Supply and demand and sentiment seem in harmony near the apex, so some small amount of buying or selling is sufficient to tip the scales and precipitate a breakout. Prices can rally or decline sharply from the coil, and the distance traveled from the breakout should be at least as high as the pattern. We'll see this with wedges in Chapter 9, but coils can sometimes become parts of other formations.

Discussions of triangles in the current technical literature will usually show three triangle formations. There seems to be general agreement that there are *ascending, descending,* and *symmetrical* triangles. In earlier

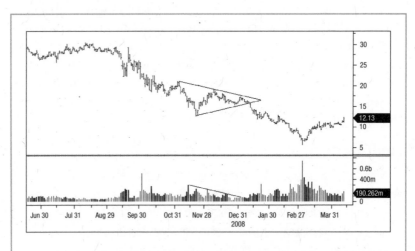

FIGURE 6.1   The triangle example for General Electric shows that
volume contracts through the pattern in late 2008.
Prices break out to the downside of the triangle
about three-quarters of the way through the pattern.

Source: Bloomberg

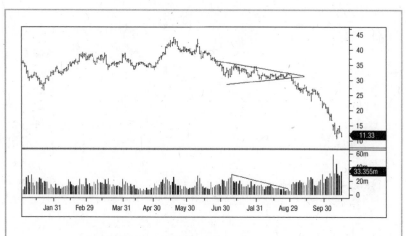

FIGURE 6.2   **Example of coil formation on Alcoa which gets close to its apex before breaking out to the downside**

Source: Bloomberg

texts, some authors talk about an *inverted* triangle as a fourth variation. The authors who leave out the inverted triangle from the discussion, often call it a *broadening* formation in a separate chapter, and sometimes they show it as both a continuation pattern and a potential reversal pattern.

The Ascending Triangle

The natural habitat of the ascending triangle should be an up trend. Ascending triangles have also been called *bullish* triangles, *rising* triangles, and *right-angle* triangles. An example of an ascending triangle pattern can be seen in the Standard & Poor's (S&P) 500 Index in the rally from the 2002 bottom (see **Figure 6.3**).

To understand the development of an ascending triangle, we'll start with an existing up trend where prices rise until they reach a point of resistance or a line or area of supply. Looking at the chart of the S&P 500 in Figure 6.3, the resistance materialized just above 1000. There should be at least two clear rallies and two obvious dips. Once prices

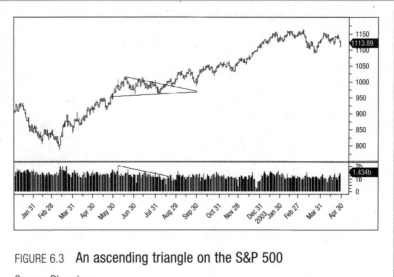

FIGURE 6.3   **An ascending triangle on the S&P 500**

Source: Bloomberg

reach resistance (or supply line), or the point at which some traders are taking profits or others are selling because prices have "gone far enough," there is a downward correction as buying enthusiasm wanes. In **Figure 6.4**, let's assume the supply line is at $60, and the first correction or dip takes prices back toward $40 before bargain hunters and other buyers renew their buying interest (support). The volume of shares traded on the decline from $60 to $40 should be less than on the initial rally to $60. Buyers return around $40, and a rally back to $60 eventually unfolds. Volume on this advance is better than during the correction to $40. Once again, traders are willing to take profits at $60, where the rally halted before. These traders could have been long from much lower levels and did not take profits on the first advance to $60, or they might have bought during the retracement to $40 and are content to take a quick 50-percent return on the rally to $60 again. Prices retreat a second time on light volume, but the buyers enter at a higher level than $40, perhaps $44. Why do the buyers pay $44 to acquire stock when they might have paid $40 a few weeks ago? The first reason is that we are in an up trend, so we expect to see higher lows and higher highs. Second, in an ascending triangle we see a pattern of

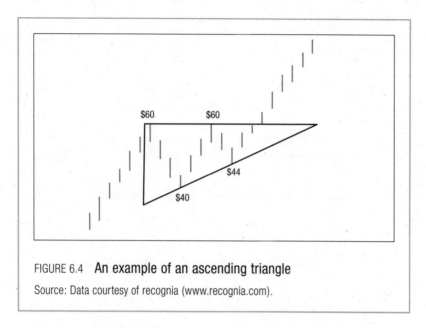

FIGURE 6.4 **An example of an ascending triangle**

Source: Data courtesy of recognia (www.recognia.com).

increasing demand, with buyers paying $40, and then $44, with stock being offered or supplied at $60. Investors and traders absorbed the available stock at $40, and now they must pay up to $44 to entice sellers to part with their shares.

Now we have a third advance from $44 to $60, which is followed perhaps by another reaction where buyers must pay $46 or $47 to be able to accumulate more shares. A pattern of aggressive demand is being outlined as the ascending triangle evolves over several weeks or months (see **Figure 6.5**). Eventually, the buying enthusiasm of the longs overcomes the supply being offered at $60, and prices *continue* the trend prior to the triangle. In other words, the up trend continues with prices going to new highs for the move up. We always must remember that nothing in the world of investing is truly guaranteed, but that ascending triangles tend to break out on the upside. While the triangle is developing, the overall volume tends to diminish, but with the volume larger on the rallies than the pullbacks.

Traders like to be involved with stocks that are making new highs, so it should not be surprising that overall volume declines during a sideways trend from approximately $40 to $60. Once prices break out on the topside of the pattern through the supply line at $60, volume

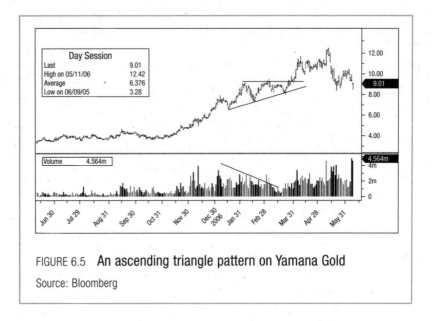

FIGURE 6.5 An ascending triangle pattern on Yamana Gold

Source: Bloomberg

should expand significantly. Volume expands because prices have just broken out to a new high, perhaps even a new fifty–two–week high. In addition to someone being a seller at $60 for several weeks or a few months, some aggressive traders may have gone short at $60. When prices trade through $60, the shortsellers will be losing money and should be anxious to cover their shorts, and this should add to the expansion in volume.

Figure 6.6 shows an ascending triangle on Lockheed Martin with a price projection; the apex indicates a peak to the price action. Note how volume expands sharply on the breakout to the upside.

Targets

How far should we expect prices to advance once they clear the sell–ing resistance at $60? The common measuring technique is to take the distance between $40 and $60, or $20, and add it to the breakout point, or $60. Prices should eventually rally to around $80. I use the phrase "to around" on discussing price targets because technical analysis is not a precise science. Prices might stop short of $80 because of a major down trendline or some resistance area, and prices could overshoot the $80

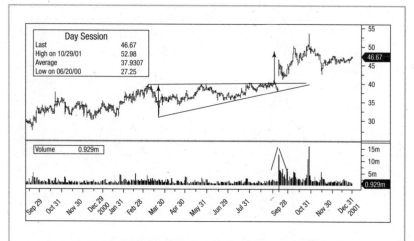

FIGURE 6.6   **An ascending triangle on Lockheed Martin with a price projection. The apex indicates a peak to the price action. Note how volume expands sharply on the breakout to the upside.**

Source: Bloomberg

target, and that would be normal behavior in a bull market. Traders and investors should consider the $80 target as a conservative measurement. The move may go much farther, and trend implications could suggest that the length of the move prior to the triangle is repeated after the triangle. Another observation worth keeping in the back of your mind is that because prices break out before they reach the apex of the pattern, they can actually reach a high about when prices would have reached the apex, thus giving you another timing tool from triangles. Another example of this timing technique can be seen with the chart of Royal Gold in **Figure 6.7**. Prices breakout approximately two-thirds through the pattern and the rally peaks right where the apex measures.

■ Tactics and Trading Strategy

Chart watchers should be prepared for a breakout from the ascending triangle that occurs approximately two-thirds to three-quarters through the pattern. Unlike the coil formation, prices should not reach the apex. By outlining the horizontal top of the triangle and the rising

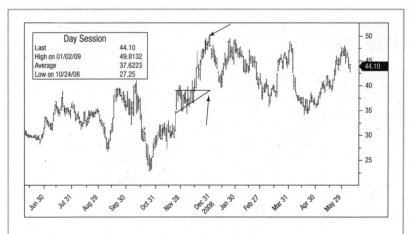

FIGURE 6.7   **A breakout from an ascending triangle pattern on Royal Gold illustrates the measuring technique and timing with the apex. Prices peak at $50—or just when the triangle would have reached its apex.**

Source: Bloomberg

lows, and projecting the lines out to an apex in the future, it becomes easy to measure and find the two-thirds point and to be prepared for a breakout. It may also pay to check the economic and corporate calendars to see if there might be any potential market-moving data scheduled for release. Traders can try to buy on the declines within the triangle or after the breakout when the subsequent up trend has been well defined. Longs at either juncture should have protective sell stops below the most recent lows to guard against reversals. Remember that we are dealing with probabilities and not certainties with all technical approaches.

The Descending Triangle

Descending triangles should appear in down trends (see **Figures 6.8** and **6.9**). Descending triangles can also be called *falling* or *bearish* triangles. With the descending triangle, we see prices already in a down trend until they reach a level where buying support develops. Let's imagine

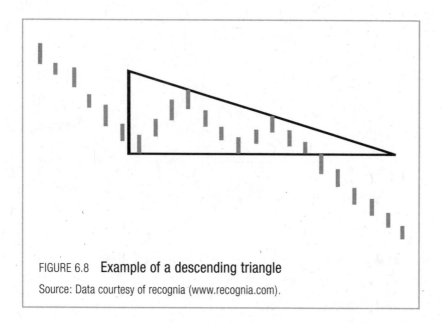

FIGURE 6.8 **Example of a descending triangle**

Source: Data courtesy of recognia (www.recognia.com).

a stock that might have declined from around $100 to around $50, or a 50-percent retracement. Buying interest might develop around $50 because it is the 50-percent retracement level, or some investors may find the level to be fundamentally attractive or "cheap." Buying interest develops around $50, and the stock manages a rally back to around $65. On the approach to $65, we find various traders thinking about their options. We might have some traders who have been unloading the stock and might consider this rally from $50 back to $65 as an opportunity to further reduce their long exposure. Other traders who stepped in and bought at $50 might seize the 30-percent return ($15 profit on a $50 investment) and turn sellers around $65. Whatever the motivations, there is enough selling around $65 to turn prices back down toward support at $50 again. Because we are in a down trend, sellers are more aggressive and volume should increase on the decline. As prices approach $50 again, the sellers are more restrained and the bargain hunters come out once more. Eventually, enough demand for the stock around $50 develops and another rally gets underway. Prices advance, but the sellers reduce their ideas on the value of the stock and the rally peters out around $60. Sellers are

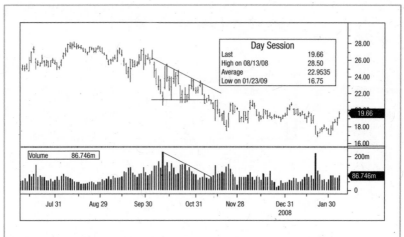

FIGURE 6.9   **A descending triangle formation on Microsoft Corporation**

Source: Bloomberg

being more aggressive in the down trend. This is the reverse of the pattern we saw with the ascending triangle. With this rally failure at $60, we see another decline toward support at $50. Support develops again at $50 from various corners—traders covering shorts at prior support, bargain hunters looking to trade another bounce to the upside, and new traders perhaps betting on a turnaround. Volume is slack on this rally, and the advance peters out at $56 or $57 as the sellers are more aggressive. The sellers capped the first rally at $65 and the second markup at $60. In a down trend, we expect to see a pattern of lower highs. Here the sellers step up the pace of selling at $56, and we find prices decline to the $50 support level again. On this decline, the sellers overcome what buying interest there is left, and prices break lower into the $40 range. This downside breakout is typically accompanied by an increase in volume. The bears have succeeded in renewing the down trend and pick up their pace of selling. Investors who were buyers at around $50 as support held now find their positions underwater, and are anxious to sell and cut their losses. Their selling adds to the uptick in volume.

Targets

How far should we expect prices to decline when they break the support at $50? The common measuring technique is to take the distance between $50 and $65, or $15, and subtract it from the breakout point, or $50. Prices should decline to around $35. Prices might stop short of $35 because of a major up trendline or a support area, and prices could overshoot the $35 objective in a bear market. A timing technique with this triangle comes from the fact that prices break out before they reach the apex of the pattern, and thus they can actually reach a low about when prices would have reached the apex.

■ Tactics and Trading Strategy

As with the strategy for the ascending triangle, traders should be prepared for a downside breakout approximately two-thirds to three-quarters of the way through the pattern. Using a mouse and cursor (or an old school wooden or plastic ruler), we can draw in the falling supply line and the flat demand line to outline the descending triangle. From there, we can easily measure and mark the anticipated breakout "zone." The news may not be in sync at the downside breakout: corporations are usually fast to release good news and slow to release bad news, so the market can break down before the bearish news might appear. Remember that people and markets anticipate! Traders looking to short this security can use the rallies to accomplish that with buy stops placed above the declining tops. Our downside price projection is the height of the pattern at the beginning of the triangle or $15 ($50 to $65).

This amplitude is subtracted from the support line at $50 to give us a $35 objective. Again, the time when prices would have reached the apex can mark a low in prices, but this is a minor point to remember.

The Problem Triangle

The third triangle on our list is the *symmetrical triangle,* which can appear in either a down trend or an up trend. You might also see the symmetrical triangle called an *equilateral* triangle. Visually, the buying and selling pressures look the same, as we have a rising demand line and a falling supply line. Prices swing back and forth in a narrowing pattern of lower highs and higher lows. In the other two triangles, we saw either demand getting stronger or supply being more aggressive. With the two trendlines marking this pattern coming closer together, we have a balance between the forces. Like the other triangles, the symmetrical triangle breaks out well before the apex. Volume should increase upon the breakout and prices should travel a distance from the breakout point equal to the height of the triangle at its beginning. The symmetrical triangle with its unique balance of bullish and bearish trendlines (see **Figure 6.10**) could break out in either direction. Because prices can break out in either direction from this chart pattern, traders should exercise greater caution and should be on guard for an initial false move or even a reversal. In a down trend, we might see prices breach the upward-sloping trendline of the triangle, and then abruptly rally to the upside. In an up trend, we could just as well see a blunted move to the upside, and then see prices reverse downward. These false moves are difficult to trade, and probably cannot be anticipated and thus avoided. Traders have a few options: we can totally avoid the equilateral triangle as one option

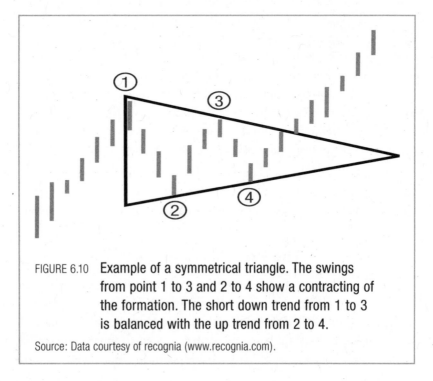

FIGURE 6.10   **Example of a symmetrical triangle. The swings from point 1 to 3 and 2 to 4 show a contracting of the formation. The short down trend from 1 to 3 is balanced with the up trend from 2 to 4.**

Source: Data courtesy of recognia (www.recognia.com).

and turn our attention to some other security. If we must be involved with this issue, we can wait a few days after the breakout to be surer of the trend and its durability. Of course, by waiting, we are giving up some of the profit potential because the stock is now closer to the projected price objective, and we could be taking on more risk if we select a sell or buy stop beyond the breakout point. This is typical of how you may have to trade returns for confidence: to be more assured in the direction of a move, you may have to get in later and forgo some of the potential profits.

Figure 6.11 shows a symmetrical triangle on the gold exchange-traded fund (ETF) GLD that breaks out nicely to the upside.

Targets

How far should prices be expected to travel when they break out from the symmetrical triangle? Like our other patterns, the common method is to measure the distance at the widest point of the triangle and subtract or add it to the breakout point. In addition, similar to the ascending and descending triangles, a timing technique with the symmetrical triangle can

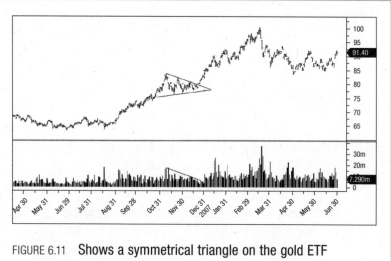

FIGURE 6.11 Shows a symmetrical triangle on the gold ETF (GLD) that breaks out nicely to the upside

Source: Bloomberg

also be found, in that prices break out before they reach the apex, and can reach a low or high at about when prices would have reached the apex.

■ Tactics and Trading Strategy

Be prepared for a breakout approximately two-thirds to three-quarters of the way through the symmetrical triangle. This breakout "zone" can be marked on the chart, and traders can be prepared for it. Because this triangle is not as reliable as, say, an ascending triangle in its ultimate breakout and direction, we would suggest that more caution be exercised. Instead of positioning a security ahead of the breakout, we would wait for the breakout before getting too involved. In addition, we would be strict in the placement of buy or sell stops, and not use a "mental stop"—thinking and doing are two completely different actions. The problem in dealing with an equilateral triangle is seen in **Figure 6.12**. Prices are in a small and irregular uptrend prior to the triangle, but the triangle

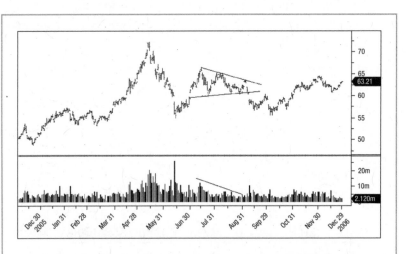

FIGURE 6.12   **In this example, we can find another symmetrical triangle on the gold ETF, but this time it breaks out to the downside, even though the immediate trend prior to the pattern was up.**

Source: Bloomberg

breaks out to the downside. In waiting for the pattern to make its decision, profits are given up with the downside gap when the lower trendline is broken.

The Inverted Triangle

The *inverted* triangle, or the *broadening* formation, has also been called a *funnel* or a *reverse* triangle over the years. It is a triangle that has been turned backward (see **Figure 6.13**). The other triangles we have covered display an overall pattern of diminishing volume and, in a way, increasing certainty and an equilibrium price. The inverted triangle seems to be a nervous pattern, representing an uncertain market environment. Prices trade in a broad sideways trend with *higher highs* and *lower lows,* with volume increasing as the swings up and down expand. I cannot imagine another pattern that would be harder to trade. Consider how this pattern plays out: we first have a rally to a slight new high, and we initiate a long position, but prices reverse to the downside and we take a loss as we get stopped out. Prices continue to slip and make a new low for

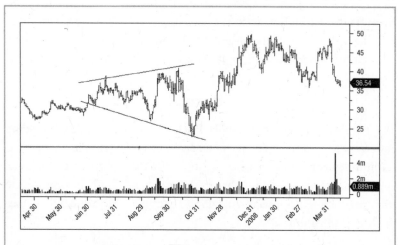

FIGURE 6.13   An inverted triangle pattern on Royal Gold. Can you imagine trying to trade this pattern in real time?

Source: Bloomberg

the move. It might not be part of their investment strategy, but some traders might short this break to a new low. These shorts prove to generate quick losses as prices once again stage a reversal—but this time to the upside. Prices rally to another new high, and bullish traders buy this new high and potential breakout. Unfortunately, this upside move also fails and gains turn to losses. Prices retreat and make a new low for the move down below the prior low. Traders turn bearish again with the new low, but they are whipsawed as prices rally a third time and break above the high seen in the second rally. This third rally is the fifth point in this widening, yet sideways pattern. Prices could make two more swings, first down and then up again, before the inverted triangle breaks out decisively. With the inverted triangle or broadening pattern, volume rises as the swings in prices get wider. In the larger scheme of things, the inverted triangle is not very useful. This pattern is not seen that often and is difficult to trade or profit from. Because the highs and lows of this pattern are expanding, not only is much of the potential target price being given up, but also the location of a protective buy or sell stop is farther away, increasing the risk.

■ Tactics and Trading Strategy

Measuring techniques do not really apply to the inverted triangle. Purchases should be made either at the lowest levels within the triangle or as close to the breakout point, with an appropriate sell or buy stop.

Boxes

The *box* formation is pretty simple. Prices fluctuate in a sideways trading pattern for a number of weeks and sometimes a couple of months, outlining what looks to be a square, with the width of the pattern approximating the height. A breakout from a box, unlike some of the triangles discussed, is usually valid. Prices continue in the direction before the box pattern unfolded.

Bull-Market Boxes

The bull–market box pattern is our basic box pattern in an up trend (see **Figure 6.14**). Prices hold in a neutral or sideways trading range before

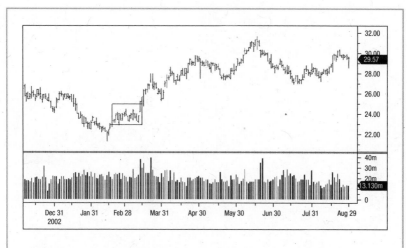

FIGURE 6.14 **A clear bull-market box formation can be seen on this chart of General Electric.**

Source: Bloomberg

breaking out to the upside and resuming the advance that was unfolding before the box pattern.

Bear-Market Boxes

The bear-market box pattern is found in a down trend (see **Figure 6.15**). Prices hold in a sideways trading range for a few weeks or months before a downside breakout occurs and prices resume the down trend.

Targets

The height of the box is projected downward from the breakout to yield our target measurement.

■ Tactics and Trading Strategy

Over the years, I have noticed that when prices break out from nice tight boxes, they most often continue in that direction and typically move quickly, reaching their target in short order. Find the target

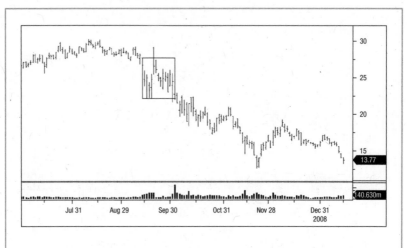

FIGURE 6.15 General Electric also provided us with an example of a bear-market box pattern.

Source: Bloomberg

price by taking the height of the pattern and adding or subtracting it from the breakout point. In an up trend, you can go long on the break above the highest high of the box with a sell stop just below the lowest low of the box. In a down trend, go short on the break below the lowest low of the box with a buy stop just above the highest high of this simple pattern.

Rectangles

Rectangles are fairly common continuation patterns and could be considered squares or boxes that have morphed into rectangles because the pattern has lasted longer, with now a bigger width than formation height. We have mostly seen rectangles in the role as bullish and bearish continuation patterns, but some analysts have marked rectangles also as reversals (see **Figures 6.16** and **6.17**). In a strong up trend, the rally gives way to a reaction followed by another rally and a subsequent reaction. Horizontal lines can be drawn through the highs and lows of this pattern. The pattern completes as a continuation pattern when prices break through

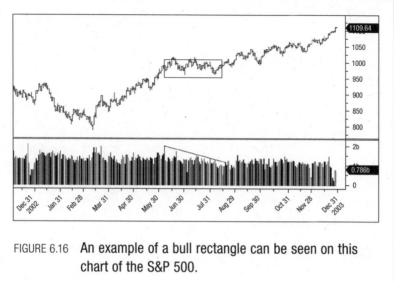

FIGURE 6.16   **An example of a bull rectangle can be seen on this chart of the S&P 500.**

Source: Bloomberg

the highs in an up trend. A rectangle reversal in an up trend is completed when prices break below the lows of the pattern.

In a down trend, a rectangle continuation pattern is completed when prices break below the lows. A *rectangle reversal* pattern in a down trend is completed when prices break off the highs. In all instances, the height of the rectangle pattern from the lows to the highs is measured and projected upward or downward from the breakout point. Volume should contract as a rectangle forms, and volume should expand on the breakout.

Targets

Similar to boxes and triangles, the height of the various rectangles is measured and projected upward or downward from the breakout point.

■ Tactics and Trading Strategy

Similar to boxes, most rectangles are fairly reliable. If the rectangle is a continuation pattern, the strategy for traders is easy. Similar to a box,

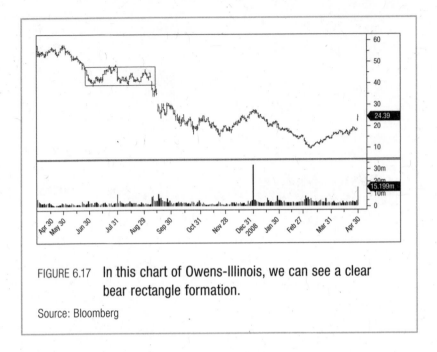

FIGURE 6.17   In this chart of Owens-Illinois, we can see a clear
             bear rectangle formation.

Source: Bloomberg

the target from a rectangle continuation pattern is derived by taking the
height of the pattern and adding or subtracting it from the breakout.
In an up trend (bullish rectangle), you can go long on the break above
the highest high of the rectangle with a sell stop just below the lowest
low of the rectangle. In a down trend, go short on the break below the
lowest low of the rectangle with a buy stop just over the highest high
of this formation.

Continuation Patterns on Intraday Charts

Even though pioneers such as Richard W. Schabacker might have gotten
a sense of intraday chart patterns by watching the tape, they did not
describe such phenomena (see **Figure 6.18**). Edwards and Magee
confined their work to daily bar charts. Probably, some day trading has
always been done by people with low transaction costs or inadvertently
by people too nervous to hold a position, but the idea of applying classic
chart patterns to five-, fifteen-, thirty-, or even 60-minute bar charts did
not bloom until the 1980s, when day traders had the data, software, and

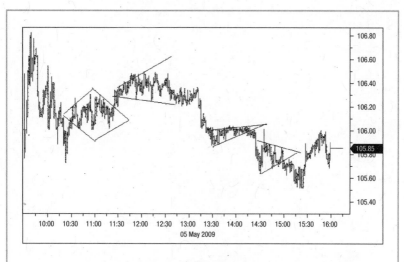

FIGURE 6.18   In this intraday chart of IBM, we can find a number
of continuation patterns that would have proved
profitable if identified in real time.

Source: Bloomberg

a low commission structure. While many technical analysts can and
do demonstrate the fractal nature of the chart patterns, triangles, flags,
and pennants are more common intraday, while normally large reversal
patterns, such as head and shoulders, and double and triple tops and
bottoms, are less frequently seen and may not reach their price targets
by the close of trading on any given day.

CHAPTER 7

Flags

FLAGS ARE SHORT-TERM continuation patterns. For this reason, we generally look for rallies and declines after the trend that was in force before the flag continues. Unlike some continuation patterns, such as an occasional triangle, the flag and pennant formations do not mark reversals (see Chapter 8 for a discussion of pennants).

It is common sense that stocks and commodities do not go straight up or straight down, and even the strongest or the weakest trends have interruptions. Each down trend is prone to profit-taking. Up trends can run into resistance and down trends can meet support. Flags are short-term pauses in the trend as the stock encounters support or resistance. If you are a short-term trader, then you need to master this pattern. If you are a longer-term investor, you'll have this pattern to use when you want to add to your winning positions. So be patriotic and wave the flag!

I first learned about flags and pennants in 1974 in a class on technical analysis taught by Ralph Acampora at the New York Institute of Finance. Ralph is a talented teacher: he can instill enthusiasm in students for the subject of technical analysis and can explain the process of supply and demand in ways that are simple to understand. I can still remember the cold winter evening in lower Manhattan when Ralph started to explain flags and the analogy he used to make his point.

Here's how Ralph Acampora explained it. Imagine you are out on the high school track in your running shorts and have warmed up properly. You start out slow, and then you sprint ahead for a

Looking back in history, flags did not make the list of the top seven chart patterns by Schabacker in his 1930 book, *Stock Market Theory and Practice*. In a 1932 book by Schabacker called *Technical Analysis and Stock Market Profits*, he does describe and discuss flags and pennants. These patterns also appear in the classic 1948 book, *Technical Analysis of Stock Trends* by Robert D. Edwards and John Magee. Edwards and Magee also note that they found that even though rectangles and ascending triangles were less common in the 1940s, flags and pennants were as common as ever.

quarter mile. After this initial fast lap, you walk part of another lap to catch your breath and rest your muscles. After this brief rest, you sprint another lap. *Bull flags* (flags appearing during a rally) are similar: a quick, sharp rally of one or two days is followed by several days of narrow back-and-forth trading with prices drifting lower on light volume as the market "catches its breath" (see **Figure 7.1**). If you keep this simple explanation in mind as we discuss flags and pennants, you should have no problem understanding this continuation pattern.

Bull Flags

In the course of an up trend or even within other larger patterns, we should expect to see bull flags. Bull flags (or *up flags*, as some older texts called them) consist of a sharp one- or two-day run-up on strong volume. Many times bull flags start with some news item that sparks strong buying for a day or two—like the sprinter in our example above. Prices might rally several dollars in a nearly vertical movement as bulls and bears react to the news by going long or covering shorts. This sharp rally is considered the "pole" or "flagpole" of this flag pattern (see **Figure 7.2**).

Various texts suggest that the pole represents an increase in price on the order of 10 percent to 20 percent. At some point in this sharp advance, traders get a sense that the rally is extended or even overbought, and they become inclined to take some profits. Although some short-term traders might view the stock as overbought, others may now see the stock as expensive and also take profits. Prices pull

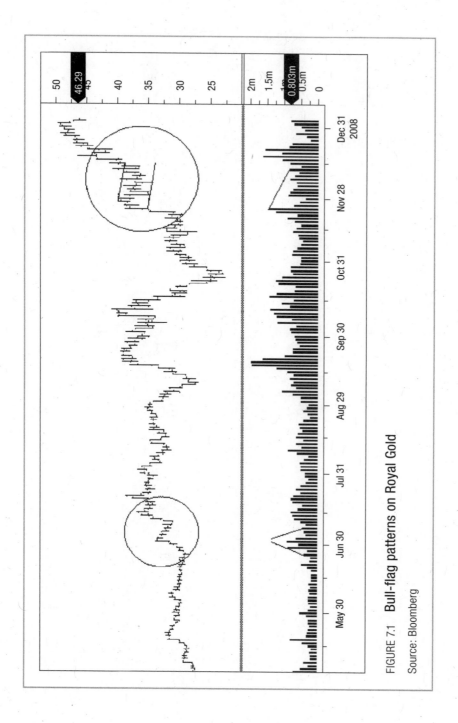

FIGURE 7.1   **Bull-flag patterns on Royal Gold**

Source: Bloomberg

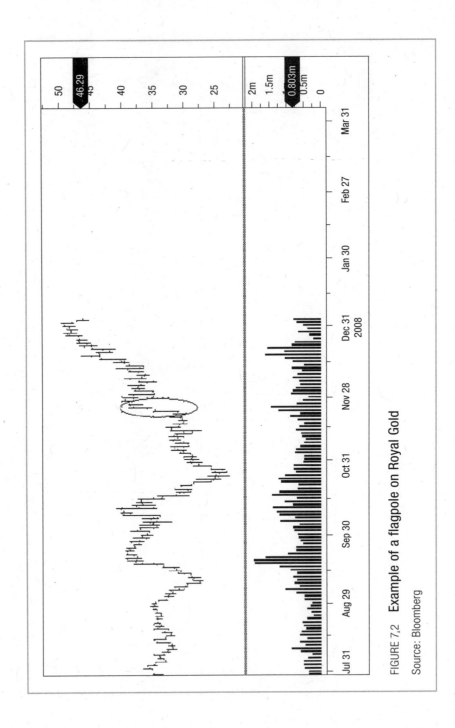

FIGURE 7.2 **Example of a flagpole on Royal Gold**

Source: Bloomberg

back a few days as the bulls take a break and maybe even rethink the news that precipitated the advance. We might have some traders who bought just before the news, or early in the pole deciding to take some quick profits on part of their long positions as well. Other older longs might also seize on the run-up to take some profits. We also might find some traders who missed buying early in the initial run-up, and they become scale-down buyers during the flag part of the bull-flag pattern. The flag might extend for four, five, or six days, or even longer, as we see alternating bouts of new buying and profit-taking. The alternation of new buying and profit-taking creates the up-and-down or zigzag pattern of the flag. The downward pattern of the flag stops when the new sellers have been satisfied.

In their classic 1948 text, Edwards and Magee indicate that flags can extend for as long as three weeks and that anything lasting longer should be viewed with suspicion. Prices seesaw gradually lower in a pattern similar to a flag that might be drooping in the wind or a loose parallelogram. Prices need to drift downward in the flag formation; otherwise, we would have a potential box formation. In general, prices might react by $2 or $3 as the flag unfurls. While flags are really most at home on daily and intraday charts, they can be at times found on weekly charts. The implications of the flag pattern are the same on the shorter time frame, but Edwards and Magee caution that what may look like a flag on a long-term monthly chart might be a reversal pattern rather than a consolidation for another move ahead. Such a reversal can be seen looking at **Figure 7.3** and **Figure 7.3a**.

It looks like the price action in Figure 7.3 in late 2001 and early 2002 will be another bear-flag formation, but in Figure 7.3a, we can see how this bear flag became a reversal pattern and prices moved up instead of down.

Some technicians believe that the "ideal" slant for the bull flag is the parallelogram slanting downward by about 45 degrees. Schabacker noted that flags could develop between strict horizontal lines, which might look like a small rectangle formation, but he dismisses this as an issue because the forecast and results would be the same. Schabacker mentions an upward-flying flag in an up trend with the flag drifting upward instead of downward. The volume patterns and the price measurements are the same as the downward-drifting flag. Edwards and

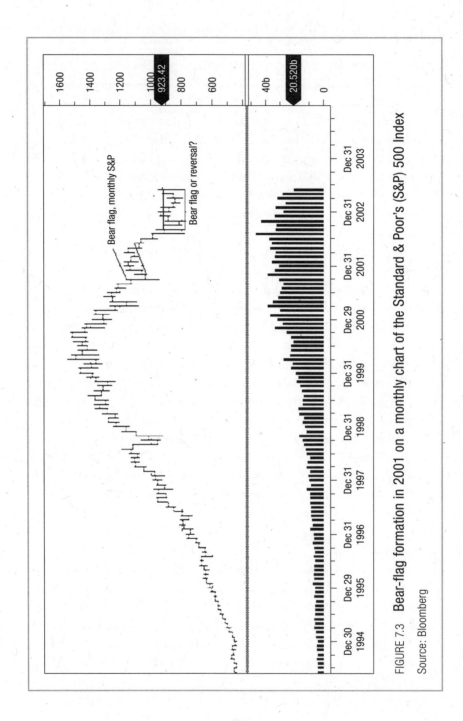

FIGURE 7.3 Bear-flag formation in 2001 on a monthly chart of the Standard & Poor's (S&P) 500 Index

Source: Bloomberg

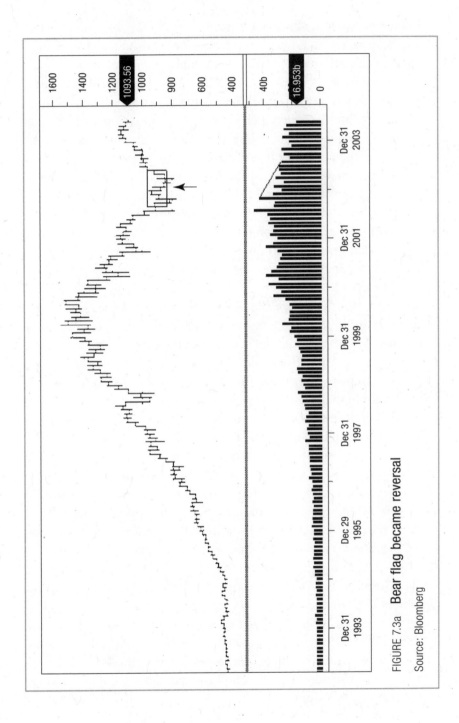

FIGURE 7.3a   **Bear flag became reversal**

Source: Bloomberg

Magee did not really discuss this variation of the flag. In a parenthetical and short sentence, Edwards and Magee noted that on rare occasions, a flag in an uptrend could have a slight upward slope to it.

If we drew lines marking the high and low boundaries of the flag, they should be roughly parallel. Volume is definitely subdued during this pullback as traders and investors are just making small changes to their positions. The new buyers do not make a big commitment because of the possibility that the pole is entirely retraced. The sellers are also reserved because they could be anticipating still higher highs. This partly explains the diminished volume in the flag. The high–low range of prices in the rally of the pole is dramatic as prices shoot up on big volume, but the price ranges in the flag are much narrower. These narrower ranges also contribute to the diminished share turnover. In a wide range, more volume can easily occur; in a narrow range, one should expect less turnover.

This is not the end of the bull-flag formation. Prices drift irregularly lower until perhaps another news item comes along to spark another "sprint"; prices then surge again on increased volume. This next leg up in the rally usually extends for the same distance as the pole or flagpole. So, similar to the other patterns we have covered, the height of the pattern is used to derive a price target. The distance traveled in the pole is added to the breakout level of the flag to project a target price. (See **Figure 7.4.**)

Note that one should not take the distance traveled from the beginning of the trend, but just the sharp trend of the pole to the first reversal (downward) in the flag. This measuring approach is similar to what would be used in the much larger measured-move pattern (see Chapter 10). Not all flag patterns will be perfect textbook examples, so be prepared to see some very short flagpoles, which may or may not have truncated moves when they break out again after the flag part of the formation. Another nontextbook issue can be the lack of increased volume on breakout from the pattern. The strong pickup in volume that technicians like to see to confirm the breakout can be absent or not appear until the rally from the flag is well underway (see **Figure 7.5**). If you encounter these exceptions to the "rule," then you should go with the price action and downplay the importance of the confirming volume.

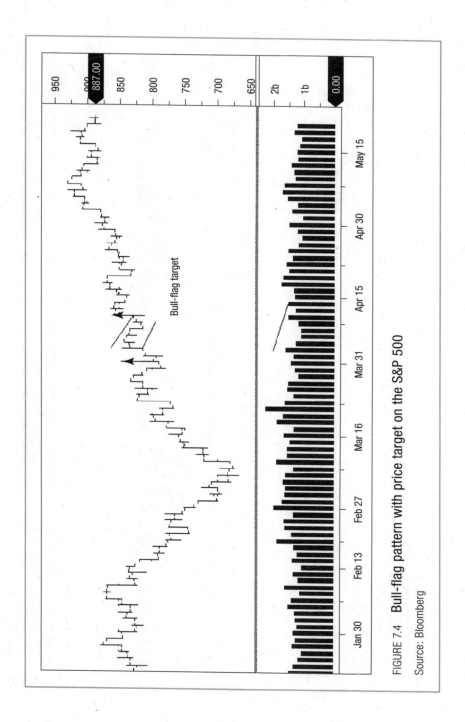

FIGURE 7.4 **Bull-flag pattern with price target on the S&P 500**

Source: Bloomberg

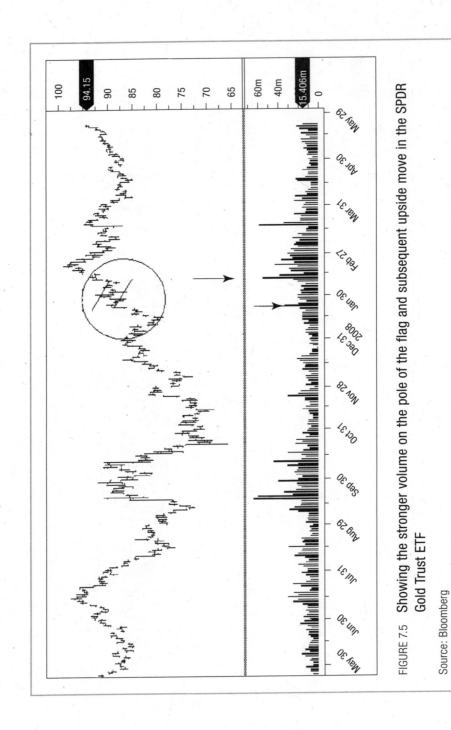

FIGURE 7.5 Showing the stronger volume on the pole of the flag and subsequent upside move in the SPDR Gold Trust ETF

Source: Bloomberg

Targets

Similar to the other patterns we have discussed, the length of the pole is used for the price target. The distance traveled from the rapid run-up of the pole to the first downward reversal in the flag is added to the breakout level of the flag to project an upward price target.

■ Tactics and Trading Strategy

In an up trend, one should go long on a break above the line across the highs of the flag, with a sell stop below the level of the lowest low in the flag pattern. This approach can be seen in **Figure 7.6**.

Be Flexible—Turn Things Upside Down

The *bear* flag or *down* flag is, of course, found in a down trend or part of another larger pattern (see **Figure 7.7**). Prices might be trading sideways or lower, and there is a sharp downside break for one, two, or even three days. Some disappointing news may have sparked the sell-off. Prices have dropped on the order of 10 percent to 15 or 20 percent, and now some traders use this near vertical adjustment as a chance to bottom-fish or bargain hunt. A limited bounce of a day or two can be seen, but renewed selling ensues and prices move lower. Another small bounce and a small dip can unfold, yielding a small parallelogram-shaped pattern (like a flag drifting upward from the low point of the pole). The up and down moves of the flag are accompanied by light volume as traders make minor moves and adjustments.

Flags, especially the poles, are fast moves, and while they can show up pretty much anywhere, they seem to be more noticeable in the late stages of a bull or a bear market.

Targets

Like our bull flag, the distance traveled during the pole is used for the price objective. The distance traveled from the sharp down move of the pole to the first downward reversal in the flag is subtracted from the breakout level of the flag to project a downside target.

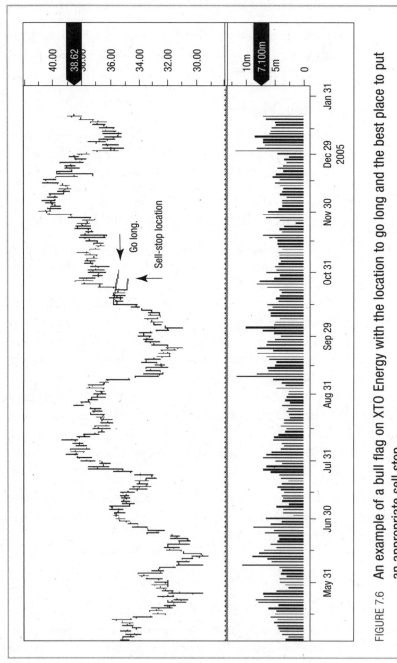

FIGURE 7.6　An example of a bull flag on XTO Energy with the location to go long and the best place to put an appropriate sell stop

Source: Bloomberg

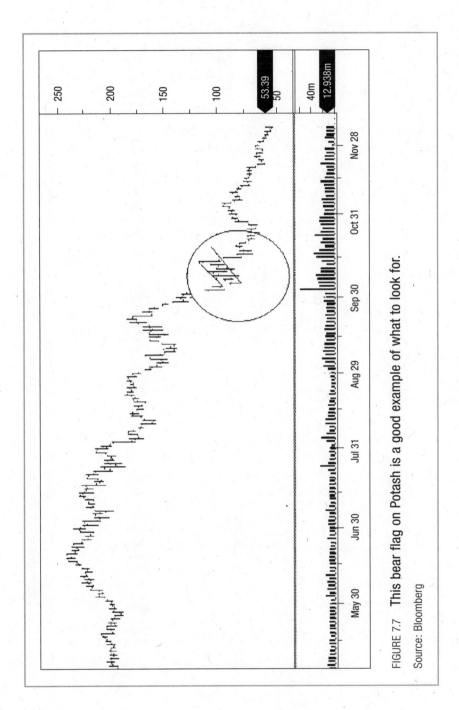

FIGURE 7.7 **This bear flag on Potash is a good example of what to look for.**

Source: Bloomberg

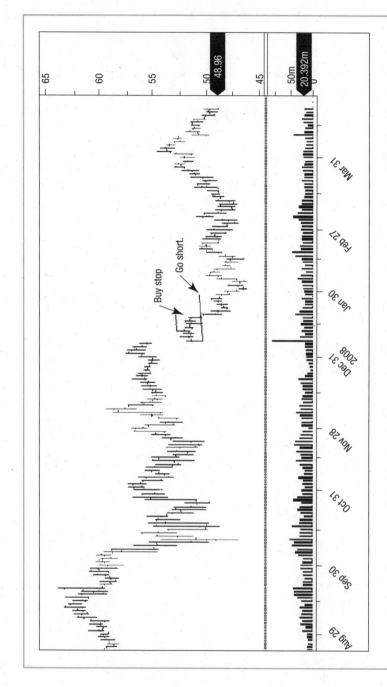

FIGURE 7.8   In this example of a bear flag on Wal-Mart Stores, we can see where we go short and where to place an appropriate buy stop if the stock reverses direction.

Source: Bloomberg

■ Tactics and Trading Strategy

In a down trend, one should go short on a break below the line drawn across the lows of the flag with a buy stop above the highest high of the flag (see **Figure 7.8**). The buy stop above the market gives us an exit point if the instrument reverses to the upside.

CHAPTER 8

Pennants

PENNANTS ARE YET ANOTHER short-term continuation pattern and very similar in concept to the flag pattern. They are loosely related to triangles and perhaps a cousin to wedges (covered in Chapter 9). In an up trend or a bull market, expect to see *bull pennants* (or *up pennants*, as they are sometimes known); in a down trend or a bear market, be attuned to *bear pennants* (or *down pennants*). Just like the flag pattern, the pennant needs to "fly" from a pole. The pennant is similar to a flag with respect to the strong and sharp initial move up or down to form the pole. However, the pennant formation has converging lines bounding the subsequent correction, while the flag has roughly parallel lines. The pennant part of the formation is like a miniature equilateral triangle. The triangle part of the bull pennant can droop to the downside or have more of a sideways orientation, while the bear pennant can drift upward or trade laterally.

The Bull Pennant

To visualize the bull pennant, let's return to the example of the sprinter in Chapter 7. Prices may be trading in a sideways consolidation or trading range, or may already be in an up trend, and the market reacts to some news that traders and investors interpret as bullish and is perhaps somewhat unanticipated. Prices race ahead, like our sprinter, for one, two, or even three days, and then pause. Our sprinter is walking to rest his muscles and gulp down air while prices correct their steep advance. This sharp advance can be on the order of 10 to 15 percent, and even

20 percent. Kirkpatrick and Dahlquist suggest an average of 19 percent.[1]
In this quick rally, prices can run up several dollars and attract some
sidelined investors and traders. Some investors may consider the rally
of the pole to be extended or overdone, and they might consider doing
some selling. Other traders may also seize on the opportunity to take
some quick profits if they bought early in the pole. Nimble traders might
even do some shorting of this rapid advance counting on some sort of
retracement or pullback. Others may be attracted to buy this security for
the first time or add to an existing long position, but only on a pullback
or some dip. The natural inclination to buy when it is on sale also extends
to trading. Longer-term investors may want to buy this security, but
only on a retracement of the recent sharp markup. They recognize the
value in the company, but are disciplined in their buying strategy. You
can see that many different participants can be acting in the marketplace
at the same time; it is the interplay of buying and selling that makes
the patterns on the graph or screen. In **Figure 8.1**, we see a bull pennant
on Verizon as part of a broad sideways trading range.

After the pole, prices trade in a sideways or downward-sloping
congestion zone. The bull-flag pattern in Chapter 7 droops in the
"wind," but the bull or up pennant can have a good breeze behind
it. (A little bit of imagination goes a long way in recognizing chart
patterns and in making them work for you.) The price action in the
pennant can alternate between buyers looking to accumulate further
shares or contracts on weakness and some short-term traders using
strength to pare positions or take profits. Volume falls throughout the
pennant or the small triangle-like part of the pattern. Bulls and bears
are juggling their positions in the days after the sharp run-up of the
pole. Some traders will be taking profits because they view the rally as
overbought or extended. Other short-term traders who blend in fundamentals might see the stock as expensive or rich and also nail down
some profits. Prices retreat or churn sideways a few days as everyone
rethinks the news or events that may have sparked the initial advance.
Opinions are not particularly strong, and volume declines as a result.
In thinking about consolidation patterns in general, we should expect
light volume to be natural within a narrow trading range. Edwards
and Magee believed that volume should shrink faster in the pennant
than in a flag formation.

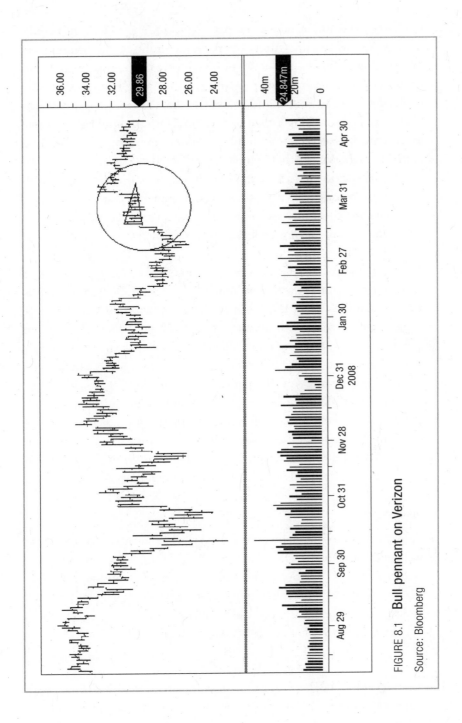

FIGURE 8.1 **Bull pennant on Verizon**

Source: Bloomberg

Early longs might take some partial profits, and older longs could also use this as an opportunity to take some profits. Other participants may get involved as scale-down buyers during the pennant part of the pattern. Prices can trade laterally in this diminutive triangle shape for a week or so, and sometimes as long as three weeks. A pennant (or flag) could extend longer than three weeks, but we should grow suspicious that the pattern could result in another move higher. If volume remains high during the "pennant part" of the formation, then we should also be on guard for a reaction in the opposite direction, instead of a continuation of the prior trend. I would interpret the high volume as a sign that older longs are taking full advantage of the rally to step up their liquidation, and the probabilities would increase that a reversal to the downside was unfolding.

Some technicians have observed enough flags and pennants to believe that pennants are more reliable than flags. Other technicians believe that the tighter the pennant, the more reliable it is in continuing the prior trend with another strong advance. The reliability of pennants might hinge more on the ability and experience of the chart reader, however. There are some other generalizations about pennants. First, the body of the pennant seems to slope against the prior trend—that is, down in an up trend and up in a down trend. Second, in strong up trends and down trends, the body of the pennant might typically be horizontal or even slope in the direction of the trend. These are really general observations without a meaningful study, and they should not affect your identification of pennants day to day.

Targets

After the body of the pennant is finished, prices break out or move out again and surge higher. The length of the pole (the height measured in dollars and cents or points on some indexes) is the minimum distance prices can travel when they emerge from the body of the pennant. Volume should expand significantly on this new rally because buyers are anxious to participate in it (see **Figure 8.2**).

■ Tactics and Trading Strategy

In an up trend, one should go long on a breakout as soon as it occurs, with a sell stop just below the level of the lowest low in the pennant pattern.

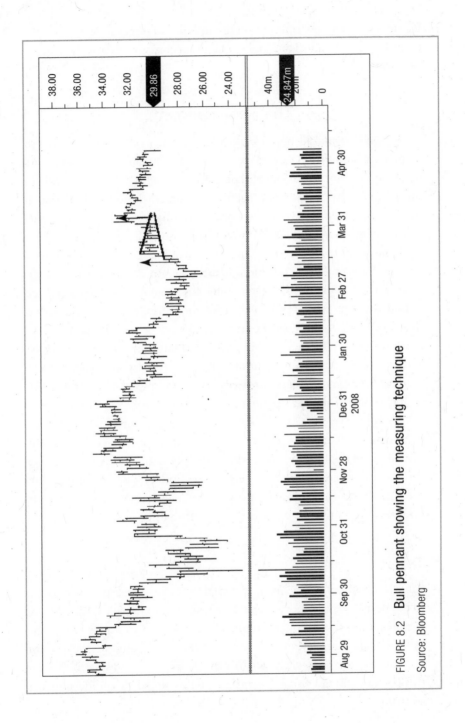

FIGURE 8.2 **Bull pennant showing the measuring technique**

Source: Bloomberg

If prices fail to follow through on the upside and prices suddenly reverse, then the sell stop cuts your losses when it becomes clear that the pattern isn't working.

The Bear Pennant

Bear pennants should be making their habitat in down trends, in top formations, and also in secondary reactions within an ongoing bull market. Bear pennants form like bull pennants, but with a sharp sell-off over one to three days, possibly in reaction to some disappointing or bearish news. Prices then trade sideways or slightly higher as the pennant part of the formation plays out. Although this also is a generalization, bear pennants seem to be shorter in duration than bull pennants. A bull pennant might take a week to unfold, but the length of the bear pennant is shorter. We don't know for certain why this happens, but our experience of bull and bear markets shows that bear markets are shorter in duration than bull markets, and this could influence someone's thinking. Over the long history of the U.S. stock market, bull markets have averaged approximately thirty-nine months, or about three years, whereas bear markets have averaged nearly one year in duration since World War II.

The body of the bear pennant has the same interplay of short- and longer-term players (see **Figure 8.3**). Some traders view the sharp one- or two-day sell-off that forms the pole as an opportunity to scalp the market from the long side or perhaps an opportunistic chance to cover shorts established at a higher level. Some traders who are oriented to the short term might be buying with a view that this security could bounce to the upside a bit after selling off sharply.

Targets

After the body of the pennant is complete, prices break out most often to the downside and move lower. The length of the pole measured from the breakout point is the minimum distance prices can travel when the bear pennant completes its move downward. We should be looking for volume to expand sharply on this break to the downside. In a bear market, one should not be surprised if this initial downside target is overrun.

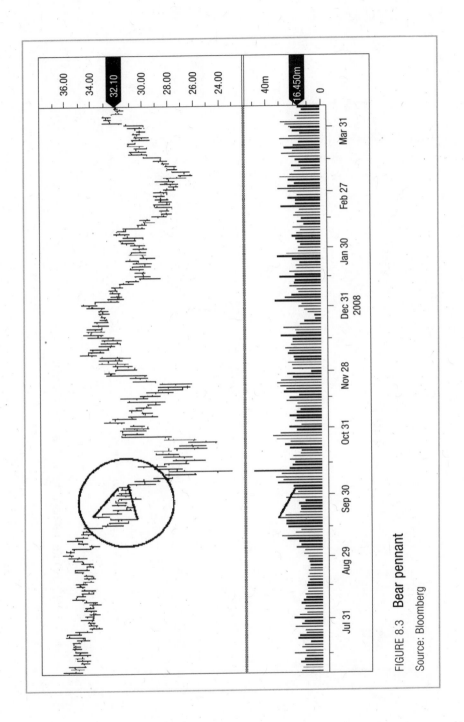

FIGURE 8.3 **Bear pennant**

Source: Bloomberg

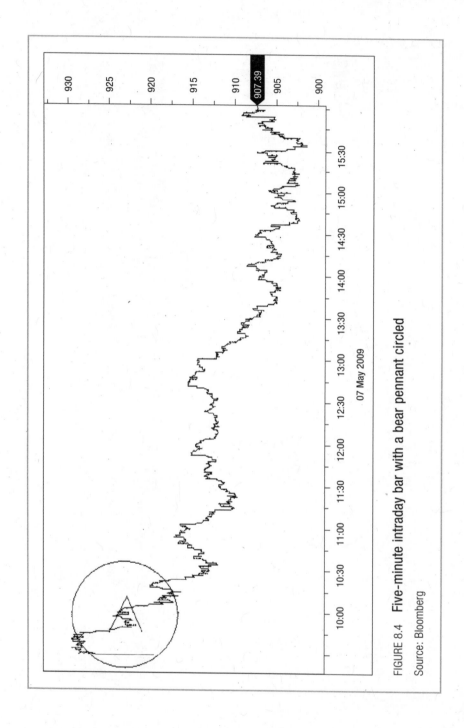

FIGURE 8.4 Five-minute intraday bar with a bear pennant circled

Source: Bloomberg

■ Tactics and Trading Strategy

In a down trend, one should look to go short on a breakout as soon as it occurs, with a buy stop above the level of the highest high in the pennant pattern.

Day Trading with Pennants

Some day traders might take a position that looking for a pennant formation might be pushing the idea of pattern formation to an extreme. For instance, in looking at a five-minute intraday bar chart, a small pennant formation will be little different from a simple triangle pattern. See the example in **Figure 8.4**.

CHAPTER NOTE

1. Charles D. Kirkpatrick and Julie R. Dahlquist, *Technical Analysis: The Complete Resource for Financial Market Technicians* (Upper Saddle River, NJ: FT Press, 2007), p. 336.

CHAPTER 9

Wedges

WEDGES HAVE AN IDENTITY PROBLEM: they resemble pennants and flags on some levels, yet they are also similar to triangles—but with a slant. Wedges are perhaps more often a continuation pattern, but they can also be a reversal pattern. Confused? Wedges come in two basic varieties that are known today as the *falling* wedge and the *rising* wedge. Texts from the 1920s described these as *upturned* and *downturned* wedges. A wedge might be viewed as similar to a pennant or coil, or maybe even a flag, except that the lines along the tops and bottoms of the price swings tend to converge rather than hold a parallel shape. There seems to be a bit of confusion—or maybe just an honest difference of opinion—among technicians about wedges. When I took my first course in technical analysis with Ralph Acampora, I learned that falling wedges were normally located near tops and that the natural habitat for rising wedges was near bottoms. Some literature shows the rising wedge subsequent to a climax peak and a falling wedge developing after a climax bottom. I also learned that wedges can become part of a larger major top or a bottom formation like a double bottom.

The Rising Wedge

Let's look at this first example of a rising wedge in the Standard & Poor's (S&P) 500 Index in **Figure 9.1**. We start our search for this pattern after a long decline. This occurs between October 2007 and March 2008. Prices have made a significant decline, and then a rally develops on light

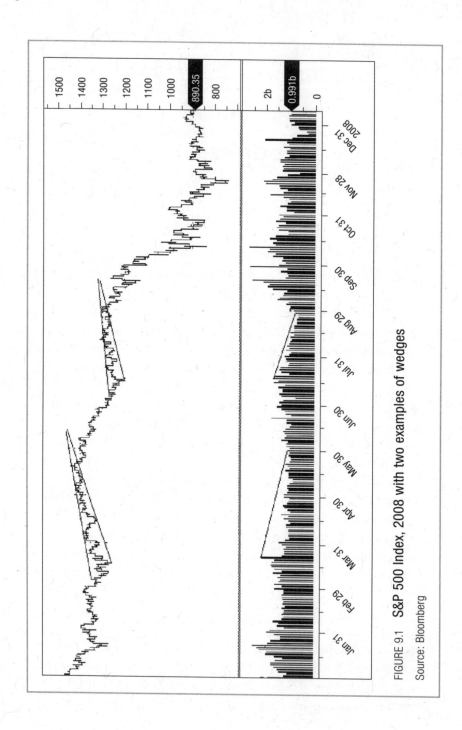

FIGURE 9.1   **S&P 500 Index, 2008 with two examples of wedges**

Source: Bloomberg

volume around March 15, 2008. Volume—or, rather, the lack of it—is the key in diagnosing the rising wedge, as well as the slant of the pattern. Prices trend upward between two narrowing trendlines. The bear-flag pattern has roughly parallel lines as it evolves, drifting upward on light volume. With the ascending and descending triangles, one of the trendlines framing the pattern is horizontal, and the other trendline moves up or down. With the rising wedge, both trendlines converge as they do in Figure 9.1 on the S&P 500, but the lower trendline rises more quickly until late May. Unlike the triangle, the wedge gets much closer to the apex before the breakout. The volume seen during the rising wedge is low and does not confirm or support the advance, which one would usually look for, to decide if the up trend was sustainable and would continue. The rally during the wedge has been on "vapors," or very light volume, and has not attracted increased volume to confirm the advance. A second rising wedge can be seen in Figure 9.1, beginning around mid-July.

Rising wedges that develop after long declines are very dangerous to new longs because prices typically retrace most or all of the previous rally in short order (see **Figure 9.2**). A wedge may take several weeks or even a few months to form, but the breakdown in the formation can be over very quickly. Typically, there is no return move as one might see on a head-and-shoulders top, and any decision to sell should be executed quickly.

In a way, rising wedges remind me of how bull and bear markets play out. It might take three years for a bull market to reach its peak and turn down, but the bear market can be over in just a year or less and retrace a large portion of the previous bull move. Rising wedges that develop after a climax peak can have an initial breakout from the wedge and then have a pullback rally before the decline starts in earnest (see **Figure 9.3**).

Targets

Wedges do not have price targets derived in the same way as the other patterns we have covered in earlier chapters. We do not take the height of the pattern and project it up or down. Rising wedges often retrace most if not all of their rise, so their price target is basically a return to where the pattern began.

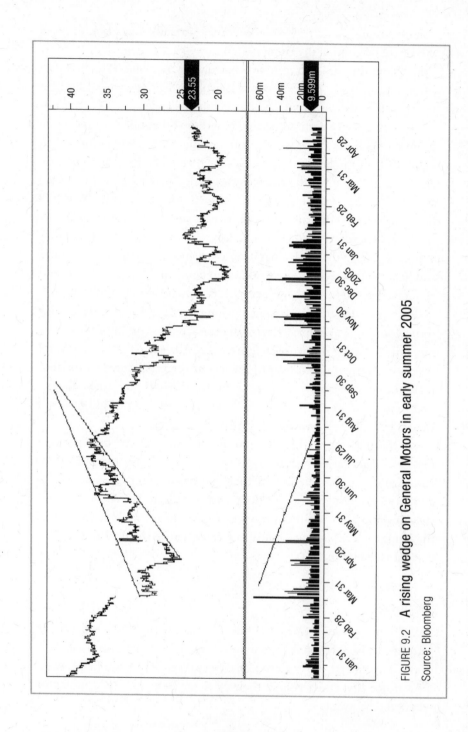

FIGURE 9.2 A rising wedge on General Motors in early summer 2005

Source: Bloomberg

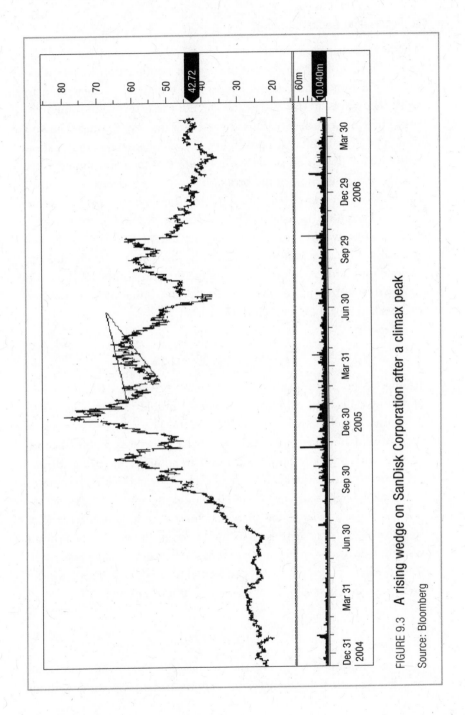

FIGURE 9.3　A rising wedge on SanDisk Corporation after a climax peak

Source: Bloomberg

■ Tactics and Trading Strategy

The way to decide whether a wedge is a continuation pattern or a reversal is to look at the slope of the pattern: continuation wedges slope *against* the trend, and reversals slope *with* the trend. Wedges tend to work themselves all the way to the apex of the pattern, but sometimes they break out one-half to three-quarters of the way through, and you should be prepared for that possibility. If you encounter a continuation rising wedge formation as shown in **Figure 9.4**, then you should enter a trade in the direction of the breakout as soon as it occurs: remember, the rising wedge moves fast. Your buy stop should be just over the other side or the top of the wedge. The example of Apple Inc. in late 2007 in Figure 9.4 would mean a buy stop around $210. If the wedge is a reversal wedge, then you should close out the trade in the direction of the previous trend and enter a trade in the direction of the breakout, up or down. Your stop protection should be on the other side of the wedge that peaked in late December 2007.

The Falling Wedge

Falling wedges are similar to rising wedges in two ways: falling wedges also display a lack of volume as the pattern unfolds, and they also tend to approach their apex before their breakout. The falling wedge that is seen around a market peak has prices drifting lower in a coil-like formation with both the upper and lower trendlines converging. Buyers pretty much remain sidelined as prices drift downward with intermittent rallies, all on light volume. The light volume suggests that investors are not particularly bearish, and prices decline more because of a lack of bids than because of aggressive selling by longs. Prices slant downward until the down trendline of the wedge is broken. Unlike the rising wedge where prices fall sharply and quickly, the falling wedge usually sees prices slowly scallop back up towards the recent highs.

The Volume Debate

For both the rising wedge and the falling wedge, the finance literature over the years states that the breakout from the pattern is "with or without

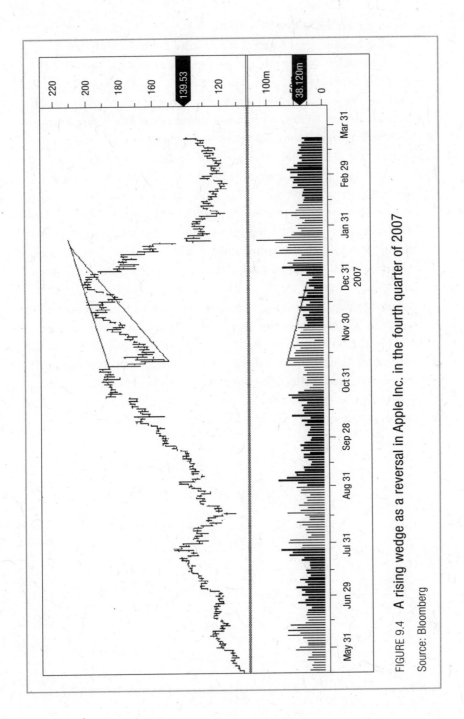

FIGURE 9.4   A rising wedge as a reversal in Apple Inc. in the fourth quarter of 2007

Source: Bloomberg

a volume increase." Obviously, this indecisive view on volume can be confusing because most patterns see increased volume with their break-outs or breakdowns. Because the wedge pattern develops on very light volume, it might be logical to expect that the breakout from the wedge would also be a nonevent as far as volume goes. It would also be within reason to expect volume to increase when prices break down from a rising wedge even if the rise was on light volume. Let's say that prices advance from $25 to $37 as the wedge develops—taking a page from the rising wedge on General Motors a few years ago as shown in Figure 9.2. Prices have rallied $12, and although this advance lacked convincing volume on the way up, there still must be some people who bought. It would be logical to expect that they might quickly sell their longs when the up trendline is finally broken. So under those circumstances, it would be normal to expect an increase in volume at the breakdown point.

Another consideration shown over the years in the literature with respect to wedges is that this pattern is reliable only when the guide-lines for the formation are strictly observed. The boundaries of the wedge should be clearly defined with the price action filling in the pattern. The wedge should be pointing sharply higher or sharply lower so as not to be confused with a triangle. In addition, remember that wedges, while not rare patterns, certainly are not common.

CHAPTER 10

Odds and Sods

ODDS AND SODS is a uniquely British expression similar to our American phrase of *odds and ends*. The following patterns don't lend themselves to easy categorization, so I am lumping a few odds and ends together in one chapter as a convenient way to cover some of the lesser-known or rare patterns. You probably will not encounter these patterns too often, but you should become familiar with them.

Measured Moves

The *measured move,* also called a *swing measurement,* or sometimes an *A-B move,* could be considered a very large continuation pattern. This chart pattern is basically a major advance or decline that is divided into two roughly equal parts. I have noticed only a few measured moves in my many years of poring over countless charts. I can remember one particular measured move in the bond market in the 1990s. This is shown in **Figure 10.1**.

Even though the measured move is not a common occurrence, the pattern should still be part of your repertoire. If there is a "trick" to finding measured moves, it is to look at the chart from a broad viewpoint. Because the pattern is considerably large, you really need to stand back a bit to get the whole picture.

Dissecting the Pattern

The first part of the measured move is a relatively long rally. Prices generally move in an upward-sloping channel. The second part of the pattern

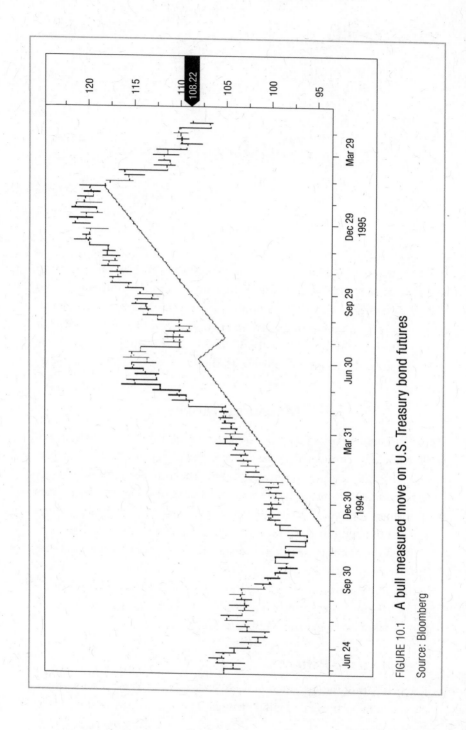

FIGURE 10.1 **A bull measured move on U.S. Treasury bond futures**

Source: Bloomberg

is a correction that can be either sharply lower or a longer sideways consolidation. After the correction phase of the measured move, another rally ensues that extends or carries as far as the first leg. The measured move can also occur in a down trend with the two approximately equal down legs separated by a rally or an upward correction (see **Figure 10.2**).

The measured move is not discussed in every technical book you'll come across, and in the relatively few books that do talk about it, I have found the coverage of volume to be sorely lacking. In the up legs and the down legs, we would want to see volume expand in the direction of the trend to confirm the trend. None of the literature seems to offer any opinion on the volume pattern for the corrective phase, and only one source noted that volume should increase significantly halfway up the second leg without giving any explanation or reasoning for it.[1] Analysts over the past eighty years have done a fairly good job with the volume characteristics in all the other chart patterns. But perhaps the rarity of the measured move and its large size are the reasons why no one has really delved into its volume in any meaningful way.

The measured move tends to be readable in the late stages of the pattern, so it is not a big help in forecasting. The pattern is largely over by the time we recognize that we are clearly in the second leg.

Targets

The targets for an A–B move or measured move depend entirely on the length of the first move up or down, which is roughly repeated after a correction.

■ Tactics and Trading Strategy

If you recognize an A–B move or measured move early enough, then you can go long or short and capitalize on what could still be a profitable trade. More often than not, someone else has already recognized the measured move and only part of the second leg remains. Though I have found a few measured moves on my own, other technicians seem to have discovered more A–B moves over the years, and their analysis is still useful. This potential problem of finding the pattern late still leaves some

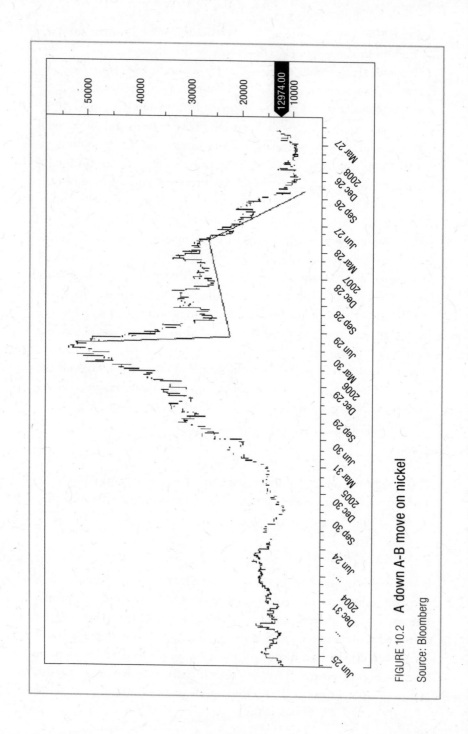

FIGURE 10.2 **A down A-B move on nickel**

Source: Bloomberg

opportunity. Look at what remains of the second leg of the measured move and then make a determination if the risk and reward parameters justify a trade. Of course, trade in the direction of the trend.

Line Formations

Line formations are sideways movements that last from two or three weeks to two or three months with prices fluctuating within a narrow range of 5 percent or less of their low. The breakout from the line formation is sudden as prices erupt into new highs. Volume is very low through the line formation until the breakout. Charles Henry Dow described line patterns in his editorials and columns that later became known as the *Dow Theory*. Dow suggested that a line can be either accumulation as in a base or distribution as in a top. William Peter Hamilton, author of the classic, *The Stock Market Barometer* (Harper and Brothers, 1922), later interpreted Dow's original editorials from 1900 to 1902. Robert Rhea was an early figure in the history of the Dow theory and started his own investment service called "Dow Theory Comment" in 1932. Rhea spent some twenty-five years going over Dow's and Hamilton's writings to further clarify the theory. In *The Dow Theory* (Barron's, 1932), Rhea noted that lines did not form often enough for traders and that some would see lines that did not exist. (Sounds like some of my students, whom I alluded to in Chapter 3.) Technical tools in the 1920s were basically limited to price and volume observations, so Rhea notes that with both accumulation and distribution occurring during the line formation, no one can tell which side will win out. Today, we have many indicators, like the on-balance-volume line, which lead breakouts.

Dow and subsequent authors have said that a breakout above the line pattern is bullish and a breakout below the line is bearish. Dow was a journalist; as such, he probably did not want to speculate or form his own opinion on the direction of prices. A good journalist tries to report what is going on in the marketplace and not present his or her personal opinion of the events and so on. When prices break out from the line into new high ground, the volume of shares traded should increase dramatically. The line formation can also develop into what some call a *long-base pattern* (see **Figure 10.3**). A line formation can be a top formation on rare occasions.

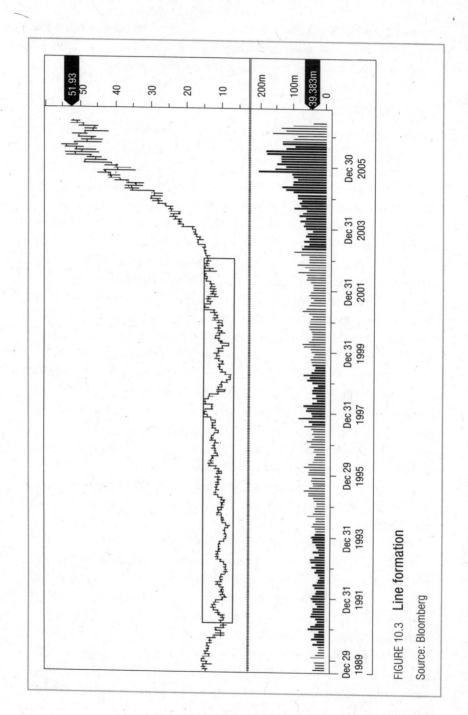

FIGURE 10.3 Line formation

Source: Bloomberg

144

■ Tactics and Trading Strategy

Traders can go long on an upside breakout from a line formation and place a sell stop just below the most recent low of the pattern. Traders should try to limit losses to just 8 percent from entry. A breakout to the downside from a line pattern could be shorted with a buy stop just above the most recent high within the line pattern.

The Long-Base Pattern

The long-base pattern exists, but seems to be just another way of looking at a line formation (see **Figure 10.4**). When a line evolves into a major bottom, it can be called a *long base*. If you think we'll only recognize this pattern with hindsight, you are correct. A question quickly arises: how long should this major bottom pattern go on? I only found two authors who address this. R. Hanson and R. Mann wrote a book titled *Non-Random Profits*, in which they outline an ideal system to make consistent investment profits.[2] They tested long bases that lasted at least eleven calendar quarters. The authors found that the median price gain was 300 percent when stocks broke out from an eleven-quarter consolidation. Once a stock qualifies under the eleven-quarter rule, it should be bought at a price not to exceed the twenty-fifth percentile of the range of the base.

Diamonds

Diamonds, the gems, are rare, and diamonds, the chart patterns, are also rare. The diamond could be considered to be both a continuation pattern and also a reversal pattern (see **Figure 10.5**). The formation of the diamond could be the result of a number of other patterns. The diamond could be viewed as an inverted triangle followed by an equilateral triangle. Or the diamond could be a broadening pattern, which after a couple swings up and down reverts to an equilateral triangle. Another explanation could be a complex head-and-shoulders pattern with a V-shaped neckline.

Diamonds need active markets and good volume, so they are not likely to be encountered at a bottom. They are often found after a big upswing in price. The public is typically drawn into the stock

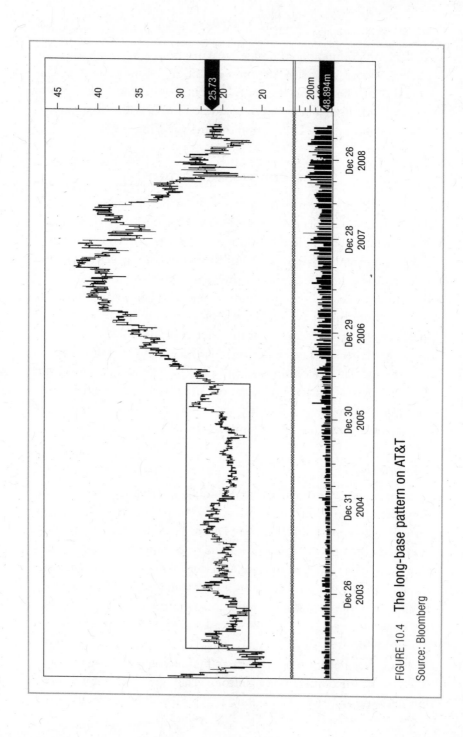

FIGURE 10.4　The long-base pattern on AT&T

Source: Bloomberg

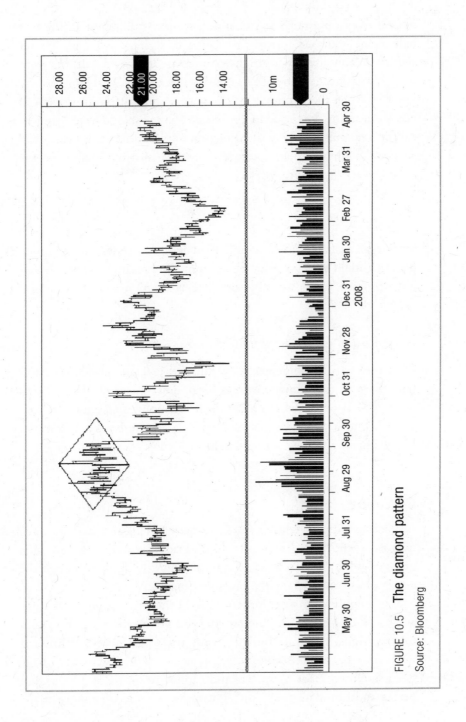

FIGURE 10.5 **The diamond pattern**

Source: Bloomberg

market after a big rally, and volume expands as they buy. In the first half of the diamond, prices first swing back and forth with greater swings up and down with high volume. In the second half, the price swings contract, as does the volume. Prices can break out on the upside to turn the diamond into a continuation pattern or prices can break out to the downside in a reversal. Volume should have a significant increase regardless of the direction of the breakout. Edwards and Magee thought that diamond reversals were easier to detect on weekly charts rather than daily charts.

Targets

Similar to triangle and head-and-shoulders formations, the diamond pattern should travel at least as far from the breakout as the greatest distance from its top to its bottom. This is a minimum distance and is likely to be overrun.

■ Tactics and Trading Strategy

Over the years, some people have found that diamonds are tricky to trade, because they can sometimes break down first, and then rally to new highs. Because the right half of the diamond is an equilateral triangle, a similar tactic can be used: go long on the breakout from the triangle shape and use a sell stop below the most recent low.

Bull Traps

A bull trap happens when a stock has been trading in a narrow range near its recent highs (see **Figure 10.6**). Prices break out to new high ground by less than 10 percent, and then quickly decline through the nearby lows or support of the previous range.

The people who went long or bought the breakout to new highs are hit with losses. The bigger the volume seen on the breakout to new highs, the more bulls are caught wrong-footed. While the bulls may be excited about the breakout, sellers who may have been sidelined seem to appear and capitalize on these new higher prices and liquidate their long positions. This extra supply at the

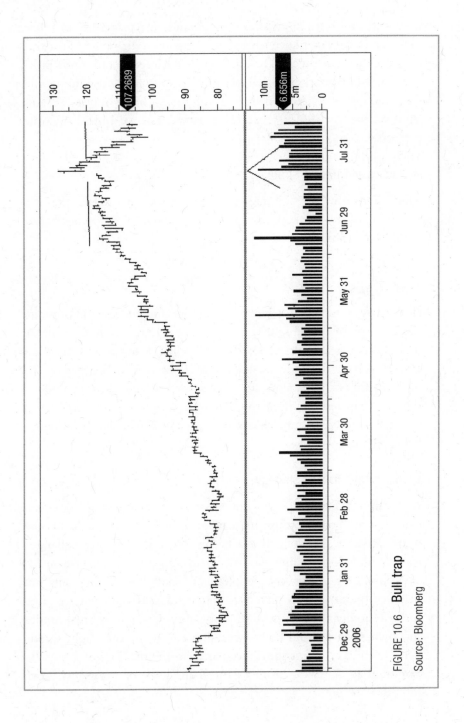

FIGURE 10.6 — **Bull trap**

Source: Bloomberg

new highs more than satisfies the demand, and prices retreat. The new longs are trapped with losses and some sell, which, in turn, pressures prices lower. The difference between a rally and pullback in a bull market is that prices rise on expanded volume and then retreat or correct on lighter volume. When volume remains high on the decline, it separates it from a normal bullish volume pattern.

■ Tactics and Trading Strategy

There is no way to really trade the bull trap except to avoid the trap. Be careful of any breakout from a pattern and use a sell stop just below the breakout point.

Bear Traps

Bear traps seem to be a rarer commodity and the mirror opposite of bull traps (see **Figure 10.7**). With the bear trap, the stock or index declines to a new low area from a trading range, but this move is less than 10 percent from the breakout point. Volume is fairly heavy on the decline. Prices subsequently rally back over the trading range. Once the bear trap resolves itself to the upside, a good intermediate term rally can develop, with prices advancing 10 to 25 percent or more if it becomes a major move.

■ Tactics and Trading Strategy

Even though bear traps are not as common as bull traps, I began to notice more bear traps, or maybe just false breakdowns, in the fourth quarter of 2008. As we began 2009, stocks and exchange-traded funds looked like they were making possible inverse head-and-shoulder bottoms and complex head-and-shoulder bottoms, but many of these patterns rallied to their necklines and then retreated to break under their immediate right shoulders. Prices break under the right shoulder and then rebound to make another right shoulder. This breakdown is short-lived and has the makings of a trap. Be careful of any breakout from a pattern and use a buy stop just above the breakout point.

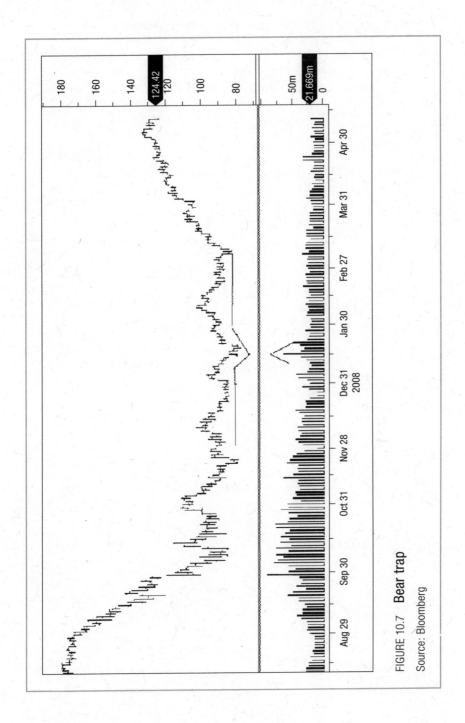

FIGURE 10.7 **Bear trap**

Source: Bloomberg

CHAPTER NOTES

1. William J. Jiler, *How Charts Can Help You in the Stock Market* (Putney, NSW, Australia: Trendline Publishing Co., 1963).

2. Raymond Hanson, and Robert. K. Mann *Non-Random Profits* (Freedom Press of Rhode Island, 1978).

CHAPTER **11**

Keep Your Seat Belts Fastened
Reversals Ahead

THERE ARE SEVERAL KINDS of reversals. Reversals are relatively quick and sometimes dramatic. There are one-day and two-day reversals. There are buying and selling climaxes and spikes. There are also a few "near reversals" to also consider. Some reversals are subtler than others, such as the close above the high of a low day. Many of these reversals can appear on the next longer time frame, like weekly charts and sometimes even monthly charts. Although many money managers declare themselves to be so-called long-term investors and look forward to holding positions ideally for multiyear secular moves, short-term reversals should not be ignored, because they can mark the tipping point for the start of a longer-term shift in the markets. Even if you decide not to act on a key reversal because you have a long-term view of the markets, then you might want to take the extra time to reexamine your original themes and holdings to see if any shifts could be warranted.

Investors seem more interested in being able to pick the top and having the bragging rights that they sold their longs or shorted the market at the top. For some unexplained reason, at least to me, there seem to be fewer investors boasting that they bought the bottom tick and rode a position up for a major rally. Typically, members of the public are out of the market at the bottom but they are attracted back in as a top approaches. At market bottoms, the economic and company news is still bearish and probably deters most individual investors. Understandably, it is uncomfortable to buy stocks in a negative news atmosphere. Only after a market has clearly climbed higher and the fundamental economic news fits the now-better tape action does the general public return to the marketplace. Volume and volatility will tend to increase when the public returns. Even if you are not one to boast, the odds are that you do want to maximize your returns, so you might want to try to sell somewhere near the top. Even if you decide to maintain your positions for the big secular move, a short-term reversal pattern might prompt you to consider selling call options against your longs or taking a trading profit. The following *buying climax* or *top-reversal day* can help you if done right: focus in on *a* top, if not *the* top.

Part of finding reversals is to learn to look for extremes in behavior. Top reversals happen when there is an atmosphere of greed and overconfidence, and bottom reversals usually coincide with fear. "Greed at the top and fear at the bottom" is a timeless description of the cycles in markets.

The Buying Climax

Start to look for a buying climax or a top-reversal day by finding stocks that have been advancing for several months. Find a stock that has made a big advance, and perhaps the general marketplace holds a high opinion of the company and the stock's future price performance. The number of brokerage firms that follow and rate the company shows this. If the vast majority of Wall Street sell-side firms rate the stock a "buy" or an "outperform" while the media runs stories about how the chief executive officer believes that "things couldn't be better," then we have two preconditions for a buying climax. This stock that has already made a major advance rallies one day to a new high for the move up, and then it encounters significant or heavy selling. After the stock makes a new fifty-two-week high in the morning, it declines swiftly to the unchanged level, and then moves down on the day. The stock continues to slump until the closing bell, and it closes well below the prior day's close.

If you slow down to think about this price movement, the big swing from up to down on the day gives a broad swath of people losses—probably many of those people who bought just before the surge to new highs plus everyone who bought on the way up and the way down on the reversal day. There is now a large group of unhappy long investors who will continue to pressure the market as they liquidate their uncomfortable losing positions. The buying climax may or may not be a key reversal and mark the end of the up trend (see **Figure 11.1**). This dramatic signal might only be an interruption in the trend higher. More time and more evidence are needed to see if the climax marked the end of the trend. A weekly close below a multimonth up trendline or below a flat two-hundred-day moving average would be two ways to potentially mark the end of a significant up trend.

■ Tactics and Trading Strategy

Because the buying climax doesn't unfold over days or weeks like the other patterns covered, the strategy to capitalize on this reversal is different. As the end of bull-market approaches or in general when prices accelerate with a steeper slope, the odds increase that a buying climax could be formed. Another guidepost in handicapping a buying climax is if all the measurable price targets or objectives have been reached or even exceeded for the stock under review. For this you need to glance back from right to left on the chart to look for triangles and other patterns that give targets. Looking at a point-and-figure chart can be another way to see whether long-term price targets have been reached. There is no body to this reversal and nothing to measure to yield a price

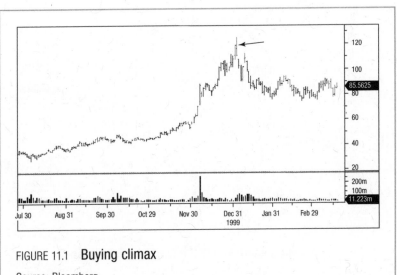

FIGURE 11.1 **Buying climax**

Source: Bloomberg

target, unlike the patterns discussed so far. A buying climax, however, might mark the start of a significant price retracement.

A buying climax might be the start of a falling wedge (see **Figure 11.2**).

A buying climax could easily occur on a weekly chart as well, with prices trading up into new high ground on Monday and Tuesday, for example, and then selling off sharply to finish much lower by Friday (see **Figures 11.3** and **11.3a**).

Selling Climax

A *selling climax* is likely to occur in the late stages of a bear market. Prices are moving down and down, and the sell-off is accelerating. The atmosphere may be such that bullish news is ignored and traders continue to sell regardless. Distressed selling because of margin calls is what you want to look for as shares leave the weak hands who are forced to sell at lower and lower prices. Logic, valuations, and a long-term view are thrown out the window. Volume should be high and is likely to be higher than any level seen for some time. This is the final washout, and patient investors with capital are there to buy these

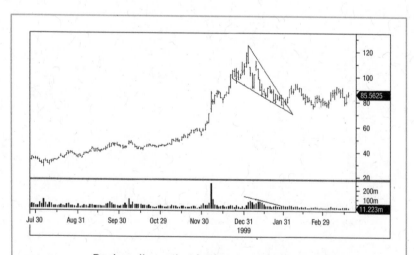

FIGURE 11.2 **Buying climax that is the start of a falling wedge**

Source: Bloomberg

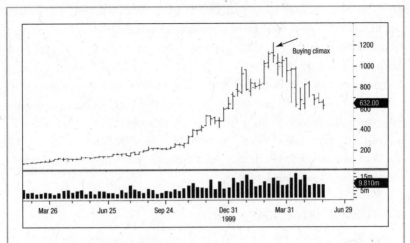

FIGURE 11.3 **Buying climax weekly chart**

Source: Bloomberg

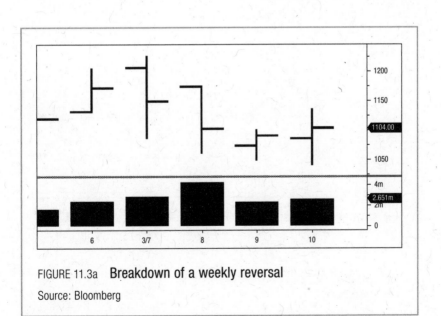

FIGURE 11.3a **Breakdown of a weekly reversal**

Source: Bloomberg

stocks at bargain, and even panicked, prices. While the buying climax just described might have been completed in one day or one week, the selling climax might extend further. It seems easier to trap late longs at a top and force them out quickly in a reversal, but once the last lot of distressed selling is over, prices don't necessarily respond on the upside. Sometimes, it takes a night of sleep before the bargain hunters dominate and rally prices. (This is not exactly the same thing as a two-day reversal, which I will discuss shortly.) Selling climaxes on individual stocks are more likely to appear when the general market is making a similar move (see **Figure 11.4**).

■ Tactics and Trading Strategy

Selling climaxes are difficult to trade if you are a bystander and difficult to endure if you somehow get caught in one. Margin-call liquidation is typically seen during a true climax, but the figures on margin debt come from the exchanges monthly with a lag. I would suggest trying to deal with a broker or financial adviser who might have a number of margin accounts in his book. A little general anecdotal information on the state of these margin accounts could prove very useful.

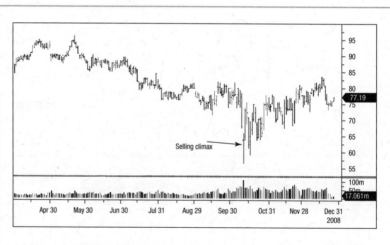

FIGURE 11.4 **Selling climax**

Source: Bloomberg

Lately, forced selling for redemptions by hedge funds might be another good marker. If you sidestepped the selling climax, then there is no reason why you cannot be opportunistic and buy with the intention of capturing a quick move to the upside as prices rebound. A one- to three-day upside burst could yield a big percentage move. One idea I found worth pursuing is to look back at the most active list from a market peak. Sometimes, the top 10 most active stocks on the New York Stock Exchange and the Nasdaq can be ones that are in weak hands and margined aggressively. These can be the stocks that suffer the selling climaxes, and you can be ready to take advantage if you monitor this list.

Spike Days

A trading session whose high is sharply above the high of the preceding and following days is a *spike high day*. Often, the closing price level of the spike high will be much nearer to the low of the trading range for the day. A spike day does not need the long advance you want to see before a buying climax (see **Figure 11.5**). The validity of a spike day tends to be seen with hindsight. No price targets are generated.

■ Tactics and Trading Strategy

Some commodity traders use a variation of the spike day or key reversal day. We are looking for prices to close weak—well off the highs of the day. *If prices close below two prior days' closes*, then it means that almost everyone who bought in the last three days is holding a losing position. Many more people will be looking to get out of their losing positions in this instance as the leverage in futures is cutting deeply into their equity. A close below two prior closes is 60 percent (three out of five days) of a weekly top reversal. If you finally react to this signal on the fourth day and sell, you are well on your way to 80 percent of a weekly reversal.

Two-Day and Two-Week Reversals

Two-day reversals can be easy to identify when you monitor sentiment along with price action. A two-day reversal at a top starts with

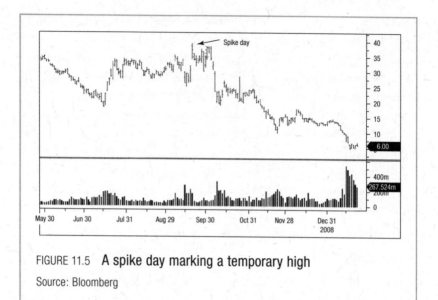

FIGURE 11.5   **A spike day marking a temporary high**

Source: Bloomberg

the first day closing strongly near the top of the day's range. This first part tells you that nearly everyone is bullish, and they have bought with the expectation of still higher prices. Overnight, a sobering reality sets in that may or may not be prompted by some news, and traders and investors are more practical, calm, and less emotional about buying this security. Prices may open unchanged or nearly unchanged, but they slip lower the entire day with prices closing relatively weak. Prices don't have to close at the very top of the first day but within 10 percent of the top, and for the down close, you only need to be within the bottom 10 percent. This reversal can also unfold over two weeks instead of two days. Prices could rally and close strongly on a Friday, only to reverse and weaken dramatically the next week. The reverse price action could evolve with a weak close on a Friday with traders and investors evaluating a new development or rethinking the current situation (maybe it wasn't as bad as initially thought) and coming back as buyers on Monday and the rest of the week. Two-day bottom reversals can be seen in **Figures 11.6** and **11.6a**. A two-week top reversal can be found looking at **Figure 11.7**; a two-week bottom reversal is shown in **Figure 11.7a**.

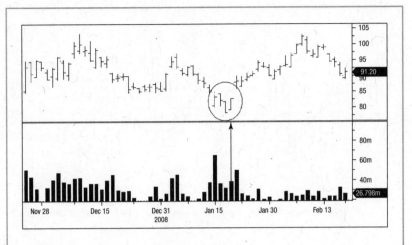

FIGURE 11.6   Two-day reversal on Apple Inc.

Source: Bloomberg

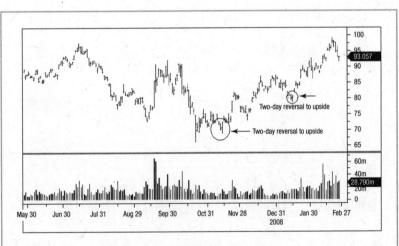

FIGURE 11.6a   Two examples of two-day reversals on GLD, the
gold exchange-traded fund

Source: Bloomberg

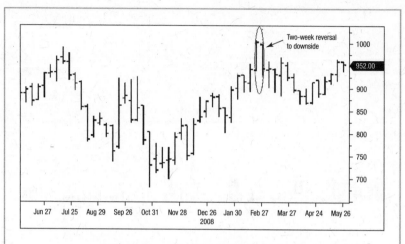

FIGURE 11.7   Two-week reversal on gold futures. The first week
ends strongly, and the subsequent week finishes
weakly, starting a sell-off.

Source: Bloomberg

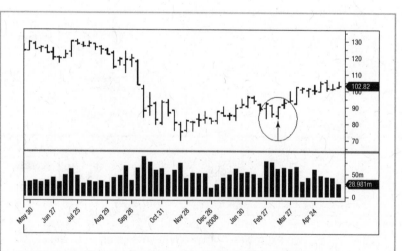

FIGURE 11.7a   Two-week reversal to the upside on IBM

Source: Bloomberg

■ Tactics and Trading Strategy

The two-day or two-week reversal should be easier to identify and act on than the key reversal day. The turn from up to down or from down to up develops over two days or two weeks, so you have a better chance of detecting this reversal as it unfolds. Reading the financial section of the newspaper might be revealing if you are on the lookout for the word *despite*. If you see that word in a headline, then you might be seeing a reversal. The word *despite* means that prices are not reacting as the journalist supposed they would. Prices rally despite the bearish news about the company. *The only way prices could rally on what was believed to be bearish news is if the news was already discounted in the price action.* Check the chart of any stocks when you see *despite* and you may have found a two-day or two-week reversal.

A Close Below the Low of the High Day

I was working for a regional dealer in fixed-income securities in the mid-1980s when I learned about this unique reversal. I worked on the hedging desk using Treasury futures to hedge mortgage-backed securities. The company was small, but the desk was busy. The maturities of these securities were different, and the coupons were often different. This meant I was trading apples and oranges—they were never quite the same. Also, the head of the desk believed in an active approach to hedging. Shorts were put on when prices failed at resistance and covered when support held. One of the signals we watched for when looking to reestablish a hedge (a short position in futures versus a long position in the cash market) was the close below the low of the high day. This reversal is just a subtle variation of the two-day top reversal, but the two days don't have to be side by side.

The stock or commodity has had a rally and makes a new high on day one. The next day, the stock closes lower without making a new high. Prices might move sideways a few more days without making a new high. When prices close below the low, when the new high was made on day one, we have a sell signal. With the close below the low of day one, everyone who bought the stock on day one and the subsequent days is at a loss. These losing positions prompt traders to sell, and a reversal from up to down takes place. In **Figure 11.8**, we can see the effect of this sell signal on Microsoft, and in **Figure 11.8a**, a similar

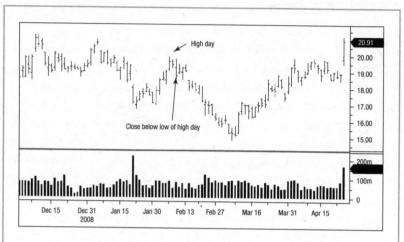

FIGURE 11.8 **A close below the low of the high day on Microsoft Corporation**

Source: Bloomberg

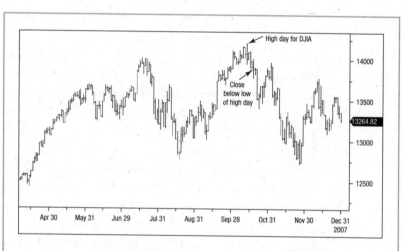

FIGURE 11.8a **A close below the low of the high day on the DJIA at the 2007 peak**

Source: Bloomberg

signal gave very dramatic results as the Dow Jones Industrial Averages (DJIA) topped out in October 2007.

■ Tactics and Trading Strategy

On the hedging desk, we used this subtle reversal to hedge a portfolio of mortgage-backed securities, but the signal might just be used to sell existing long positions instead of hedging a position. If no position existed, then a short position could be established. The reversal is good unless prices make a new high close. If a new high is made before the close below the first low, then the signal is delayed and the pattern starts over again.

A Close Above the High of the Low Day

This is the mirror of the close below the low of the high day. This reversal marks a tradable low. The security declines and makes a new low on day one. The next day, the security firms up without making a new low for the move down. We could have a few sideways days, but eventually, we could see a rally over the high of day one. When prices close above the high of the low day, we have a buy signal. Shorts will be eager to cover, and prices should respond on the upside. This technique (see **Figure 11.9**) caught the low in Microsoft in early March 2009 as the stock began a strong upside rally. In **Figure 11.9a**, the same tool was very effective with the S&P 500, catching the start of a 40-percent markup.

■ Tactics and Trading Strategy

If you are looking for a simple "trigger" to go long, then this is the pattern for you. The pattern is quick and simple. If you happen to be short, you should cover, and if you have no position—neither long nor short—then you can consider this a relatively low-risk buying opportunity. Longs can be entered using a new low close as your stop-out point.

Outside Days

An *outside day* is simply a day on which the high–low range of the current day's trading eclipses or is outside of the prior day's range. Today's

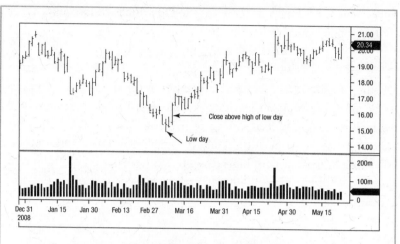

FIGURE 11.9　A close above the high of the low day can be seen on Microsoft Corporation and marks an effective turning point on the stock.

Source: Bloomberg

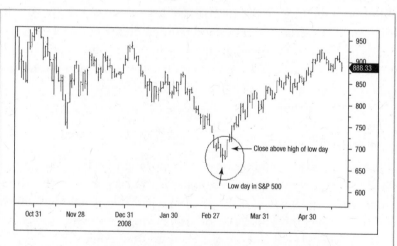

FIGURE 11.9a　This close above the high of the low day gave a very quick buy signal on the Standard & Poor's 500 Index that preceded a 40-percent advance.

Source: Bloomberg

high and low are higher and lower than yesterday's. Outside days come in two flavors: days on which the outside closes higher than the prior day and days on which it closes lower. The location of an outside day is important. If we have an outside day when prices are in a sideways consolidation like a rectangle, we'll find little importance. If we find an outside day after a good trend, then it can foreshadow a reversal. Outside days are what I like to call *near reversals*. Prices are not reversing from down to up or up to down, but something is different and the prior trend has lost some steam.

Let's consider an example with prices rallying. A normal high–low range is observed on day one. Day two brings a wide range with prices breaking above the high of day one *and* below the low of day one. Here we have the bulls taking control of part of the session and the bears also taking control with prices breaking yesterday's low. This doesn't really mark a reversal, but sets up the conditions where a reversal can take place. Day three could tip the scales downward, or the up trend could be refreshed with prices moving to a new high. Whatever happens, the outside day should be monitored like the one on General Motors in **Figure 11.10**. The reverse, of course, could play

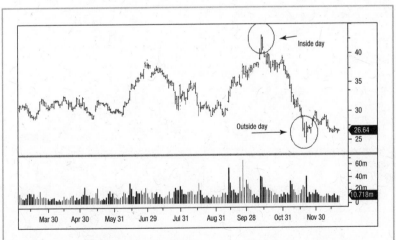

FIGURE 11.10 **An outside day marks a temporary low in General Motors.**

Source: Bloomberg

out in a down trend. From years of trading futures, I am sensitive to outside days, but the pattern will also appear on weekly charts.

■ Tactics and Trading Strategy

If you are trading on margin or any leveraged instruments, then watch for outside days: the pattern isn't moving any faster, but the money must be watched more closely. The outside day is a near reversal and can sometimes precede a true reversal. You don't have to act on this pattern, just pay closer attention.

Inside Days

Inside days are another pattern to watch more closely. In its simplest form, the inside day has a lower high and a higher low than the previous day. An inside day really means that neither the bulls nor the bears have the upper hand in the direction of the trend. After an up trend, the inside day means the bulls are losing their vigor—prices couldn't push to a new high as in **Figure 11.11**. In a down trend, the inside

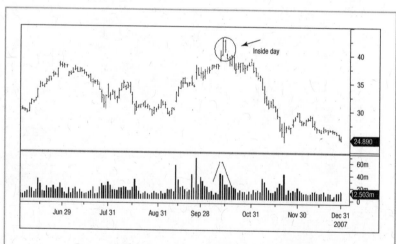

FIGURE 11.11   **Using General Motors again, we can see a dramatic inside day that happened to mark a significant high.**

Source: Bloomberg

day means the bears are weakening—prices did not make new lows. Watch the next move up or down; this might decide the market's direction.

■ Tactics and Trading Strategy

The inside day may be the market's way of catching its breadth and may not mark a reversal. Prices could just be unwinding an overbought or oversold condition, and the trend could resume. The amber or yellow traffic light is on: we probably want to brake, but it is not clear that the trend has stopped.

The Island Reversal

Islands can bring up many associations, from vacations to isolation to contemporary television shows, but here we associate islands with reversals. An island reversal is a short consolidation, typically of a few days, that is preceded by and ended by a gap (see Chapter 12). In a mature up trend, we can have prices gap up with a price void from the high of one day to the low of the first day of the island. Prices can trade sideways in a narrow range for a few days or even a few weeks, but there is eventually a gap to the downside. These few days stand out on the chart because there is no price action linking them to the prior and subsequent trend as we see in **Figure 11.12**. The concept here is similar to a two-day or two-week reversal. Prices gap up in response to some bullish news, perhaps, and then prices gap down in reaction to some disappointment. The island reversal can also be mapped in a down trend, with prices first gapping down and later gapping upward as in **Figure 11.13**.

■ Tactics and Trading Strategy

Island reversals tend to occur after a long up trend or down trend, and trading them is difficult. Because there really isn't much breadth or depth to the island, the island reversal tends not to travel all that far after being spotted. Traders need to wait until the second appears, and probably should look to add additional tools to be successful. The breaking of a relatively short moving average or a trendline would help. A buy

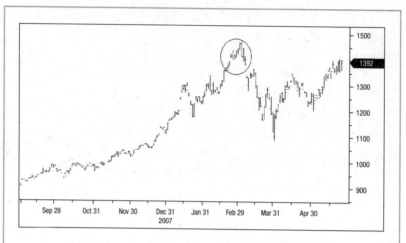

FIGURE 11.12 Island reversal on soybeans after a long rise

Source: Bloomberg

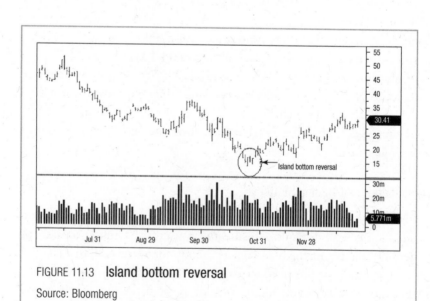

FIGURE 11.13 Island bottom reversal

Source: Bloomberg

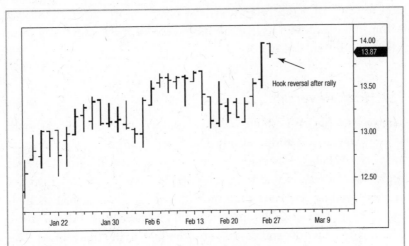

FIGURE 11.14   **A hook reversal on sugar futures**

Source: Bloomberg

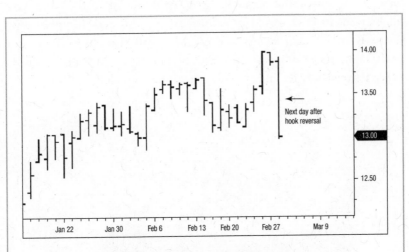

FIGURE 11.15   **Sometimes what happens after a hook reversal can be dramatic. Our hook reversal in sugar futures resulted in a very sharp sell-off.**

Source: Bloomberg

stop for an island top reversal can be placed above the extreme day within the island. For an island bottom reversal, a sell stop can go just below the extreme of the island.

The Hook Reversal

The *hook reversal* has nothing to do with pirates but sounds like it should follow a discussion about islands. The hook reversal is a very specific inside day. When we look at an up trend, we see that the hook reversal begins with a session that has a lower high and a higher low than the previous trading day. Also, the inside day needs to open near its high and close near its low. The opposite would be needed in a down trend: opening near the low and closing near the high as in **Figure 11.14**. The hook is not a clear reversal, but the up trend or down trend is almost stopped, and this can be the start of a true reversal as in **Figure 11.15**.

■ Tactics and Trading Strategy

Trying to remember the hook reversal on top of all the other patterns may be too much, but a quick survey of the chart of the stock you might want to trade could reveal how useful this and the other near reversals are. If near reversals don't jump off the chart, then, as a practical matter, pay less attention to them. The point is not to know every pattern, but to know a few patterns really well.

CHAPTER 12

Gaps

IN A STRICT SENSE, gaps are not chart patterns at all, but really nonpatterns or patterns that are not really there. Gaps are actually price voids. In the past couple of years, we have seen more gaps, I think, than in perhaps the previous ten or twenty years. That statement may be a bit of an exaggeration, but the point is that both upside and downside gaps have been seen with increasing regularity. Despite the apparent loss of volume on the floor of the New York Stock Exchange, there seems to be enough volume to power gaps. Anyone "in the business" has been well aware of the large hedge funds that dominate trading today. With hedge funds and other traders reacting quickly to bullish and bearish events or surprises, it is no wonder that prices can be sharply higher or lower on the opening. Over the years, traders have always been aggressive, but it seems like the stakes of being wrong have gone up, and quick reactions to the news can make the difference between profits and losses.

It's What's Not There That Counts

There are a number of gaps, some important and others having no meaning whatsoever. For us to truly understand the gaps that do count, we need to discuss briefly the ones that are inconsequential.

Gaps or price voids can occur because a stock is thinly traded. There are many listed stocks that have a small float or a limited number of shares outstanding. A large order to buy or sell on the opening can create a gap or void to the upside or the downside in a thinly traded stock.

If the order to buy or sell was instead "worked" slowly, the gap may not have occurred. Working an order may give the buyer or seller a better execution, but in the age of electronic trading, we are likely to see more orders executed with a mouse click with the assumption of liquidity. Some stocks are thin because they are American Depositary Receipts for companies whose main volume and activity and trading are twelve or fourteen hours away. It is easy for a security to make a gap up or down when the bulk of the trading volume is in another financial center. Traders half a day away are trying to quickly make up for the time factor. Prices gap up or down to match the overseas quote and then prices can move about based on any new information and order flow thereafter.

Companies that declare dividends can have a downside gap when their stock goes ex-dividend. "Going ex-" means that the dividend is being paid and the stock price is adjusted lower the following day. There can be common gaps within larger price patterns and gaps that are small in comparison to the price level; neither of these gaps is significant. A $1 gap on the price of gold or platinum, which trade near $1,000 and $2,000 per ounce, is not meaningful. Gaps between trading sessions for twenty-four-hour markets, as when floor trading ends and electronic trading begins, are also not usually important.

The three gaps to pay attention to are the *breakaway*, *runaway*, and *exhaustion gaps*. Although gaps can be seen on weekly and even monthly bar charts, they disappear on line (or close-only) charts and point-and-figure charts. A price gap in an up trend is measured from the highest price on the day before the gap to the lowest price seen on the day of the gap or price void. A gap in a down trend is measured from the lowest price on the day before the gap to the highest price seen on the day of the gap. Because of its construction, a gap seen on a weekly chart would have to be from Friday's highest price to the lowest price on Monday.

Breakaway Gaps

The breakaway gap is probably the most important gap to recognize, and perhaps the most useful to investors, because it can indicate the beginning of a major move. Thinking back to the chapters on major tops and bottoms, breakaway gaps can occur when a pattern has been completed. Prices could gap above the neckline of an inverse head-and-shoulders bottom or gap down from a triple top. Breakaway gaps typically occur on heavier than normal volume, and many times, do not get filled. A gap gets filled when prices trade into the price void. Breakaway gaps in commodity trading often happen because of a shift in supply. Demand for commodities tends to change slowly with population growth and growth in disposable income. Shifts in supply tend to be overnight surprises when crop reports are released. Prices gap up or down in response to the news. Examples of this can be seen in **Figures 12.1** and **12.2.** Breakaway gaps in equities tend more to be a shift in demand. Prices adjust with a gap to a takeover bid, a share buyback announcement, or something like beating an earnings estimate.

■ Tactics and Trading Strategy

A breakaway gap can be a pleasant surprise or a rude awaking, depending on your position. If you are long on a stock in a base pattern and it gaps higher to start a strong up trend, then you are probably in the driver's seat. If you are long, you only need to worry about where to buy more. If you have no position, then you want to find a spot to jump in. If you are short, you want to cover as best as possible. On the trading desk where I learned about the close below the high day, I also learned to divide the breakaway gap by two and to use scale-down buy orders to get long or to cover shorts. The breakaway gap that is accompanied by high volume might not dip at all, but there are enough occasions after the first trade of the gap that some profit-taking occurs and prices dip a little. This small intraday pullback can occur if aggressive short-term traders decide to book some quick profits if they went long ahead of the gap. If prices continue to move higher, you need to buy at the market; otherwise, try to use a partial filling of the gap to your advantage.

Runaway Gaps

Runaway gaps or measuring gaps, as they are also known, occur in the course of an established up trend or down trend. These up trends and down trends are usually pretty strong with only shallow, minor corrections along the way. Prices are in a clear trend up or down, and then a gap appears because of a fresh piece of bullish or bearish news. **Figure 12.3** shows that these gaps tend to occur in the middle

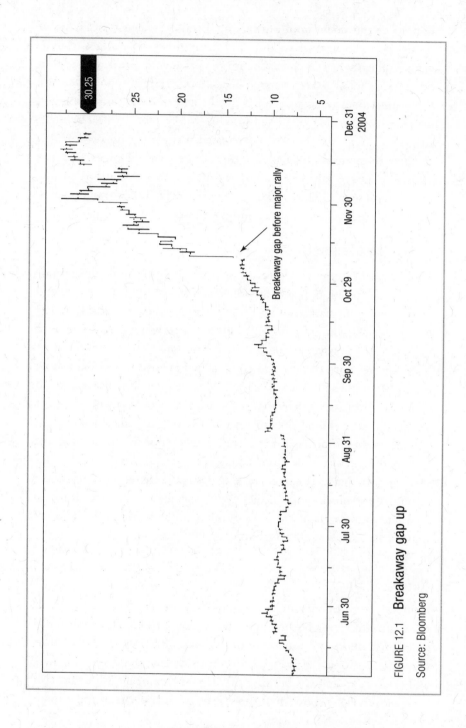

FIGURE 12.1   **Breakaway gap up**

Source: Bloomberg

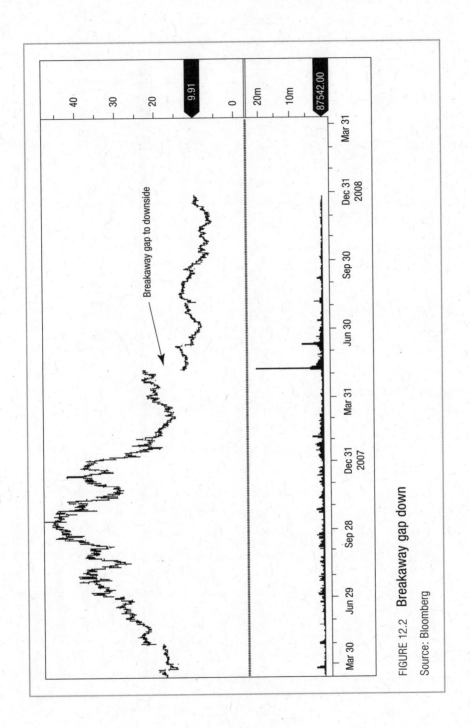

Breakaway gap to downside

FIGURE 12.2 **Breakaway gap down**

Source: Bloomberg

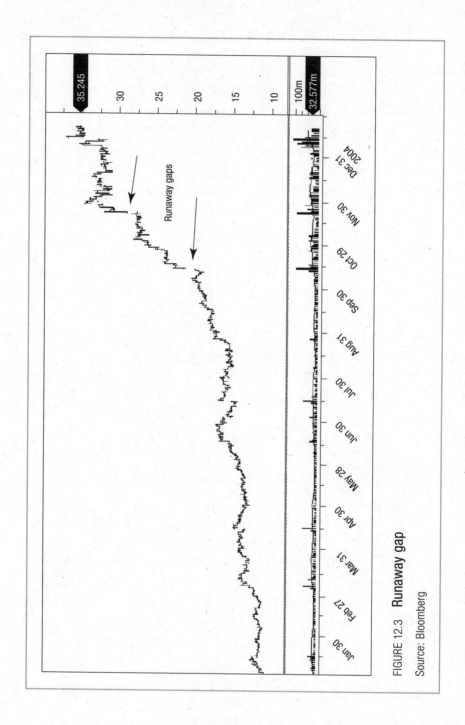

FIGURE 12.3 **Runaway gap**

Source: Bloomberg

of a move. By measuring the length of the move before the gap and adding the distance in points to the other end of the gap, you can project a major move.

■ Tactics and Trading Strategy

Runaway gaps appear with fair regularity, so traders should capitalize on them when they encounter them. The measuring technique works more often than not.

Exhaustion Gaps

Exhaustion gaps appear at the end of major up and down moves. Prices go up and up, with some traders out and looking for a retracement to buy and other traders short and looking for a dip to cover. Both of these groups hang on and, at the worse possible time, they both blink. The traders who keep hoping for a pullback to buy just give up and go to the market. The short sellers who stubbornly hope for a dip to cover just give up and also go to the market. The combination of these two forces generates the exhaustion gap. The exhaustion gap tends to be filled quickly and signals a potential trend reversal. After all those stubborn longs and shorts are satisfied, who else is left? When the buying is exhausted, the rally is close to an end.

Exhaustion gaps can and do appear near the end of down trends. Prices sink and sink, and stubborn longs hang on and on until they finally throw in the towel and dump their positions. The final purge of the longs creates the gap to the downside; because the selling is exhausted, the gap is soon filled as in **Figure 12.4** on Starbucks.

■ Tactics and Trading Strategy

It is important to know that exhaustion gaps develop near the end of major trends. An exhaustion gap in a mature up trend can alert you to a top pattern, and an exhaustion gap late in a down trend can foreshadow a future bottom or base.

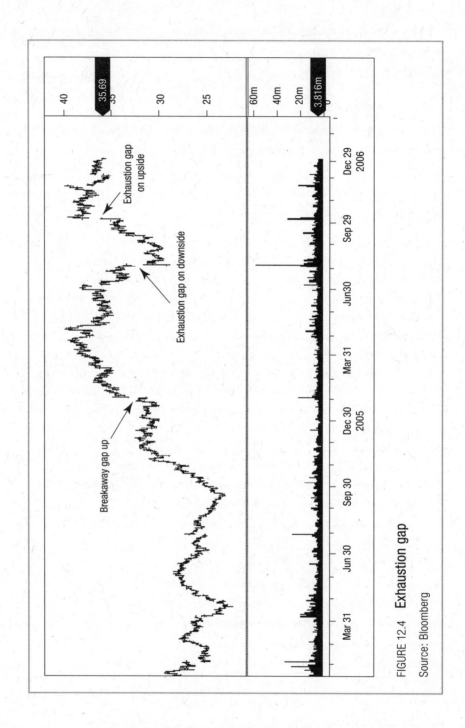

FIGURE 12.4 Exhaustion gap

Source: Bloomberg

CHAPTER 13

The Future of Chart Patterns

WHO REALLY KNOWS WHAT the future holds? Technical analysts can see trends in prices and volume and make educated guesses, and perhaps, assign probabilities to possible future events, such as price targets and cycle lows. But do we *really* know? In addition to price trends, we can look at demographic trends and intermarket analysis to add color to our forecasts. Some people, such as Faith Popcorn, can entertain or even educate us on the commercial trends they see developing. Some technicians, such as Robert Prechter, look to tie in social trends and economics in a cohesive approach to the markets. So, without consulting the oracle of Delphi, or using a crystal ball or tarot cards, can we see what the future holds for chart patterns? I believe I can offer three possible trends for the future of chart patterns.

The first option is to continue as we have been doing for more than one hundred years. Some investors will like and use pattern recognition, and they will get better with it the more they apply it. They may not rack up ten thousand hours and be "outliers," but they will probably become proficient enough that it dominates their approach to investing. As traders such as Nassim Taleb get people to reexamine their flawed risk models and think about perhaps a more practical observation-driven approach to trading, more traders could take up technical analysis and learn to appreciate the chart as at least a road map and maybe more. Others probably won't do well with patterns no matter how much time they invest. Some people have a knack for seeing patterns, and some don't. Those who don't get the hang of it will eventually drift off to other approaches or only consult the charts when the stock they are long on goes down despite the compelling fundamental story. Though I want people to respect the craft of technical analysis and to apply our tools, I also don't want the field to be too crowded.

It is very obvious to many traders and technicians that volume is a growing problem, or perhaps, a disappearing problem. Recently, I have heard financial engineers call it a *lumpy* volume pattern. In the 1980s, the problem was program trading. Waves of buy programs and sell programs would move the market irregularly, and technicians and nearly everyone else had a hard time dealing with those movements. Today, you can find a lot of people complaining about exchange-traded funds, off-exchange products, and algorithmic trading. Many times, there is some serious illiquidity with various transactions. Some market observers anticipate that new market regulations and a desire to have greater transparency will mean that volume will return to the traditional stock-exchange trading floor. Others expect that the floors will disappear and all trading will be totally electronic. Regardless of the final outcome, over time, less attention will be paid to volume and the focus will only be on price. Analysis of price patterns without the aid of volume will probably mean that we'll have to become comfortable buying breakouts without seeing volume really expand. As traders or investors, we'll have to adapt in at least two ways. First, we might use percentage triggers to enter a breakout without volume. For example, if prices go through the neckline by 3 percent, let's say, we will go long. The 3-percent "filter" replaces the confidence gained from strong volume. Second, we'll have to be particularly careful and diligent about entering stop-loss orders. Without a clear picture about volume, we might react to false breakouts and traps, and thus the key to winning and losing will be risk control. While the goal of trading from a technical perspective is profitability, the best forecast might not be the one that seems most accurate, but the one that is most profitable. We might also think about this observation by Richard Wyckoff in his *Course in Stock Market Science and Technique*, published by the Stock Market Institute, 1931, volume 1, pages 2 and 3:

> There is mechanical technical analysis and there is judgmental technical analysis. The mechanical approach is by far the easier of the

two to understand and utilize. Unfortunately it is far less reliable than the second approach. The mechanical approach relies on observation. The judgment approach also depends on observation, but the difference is in what is being observed. With a mechanical approach, patterns are being observed. Develop a model or pattern and look for as many instances as you can find. The judgmental approach begins with a set of principles. The observation that is done is aimed at finding these principles at work in the market. Adhering to a principle is more difficult than looking for formations.

A second option could be a move toward more objective measures and computer-generated signals. Some people already believe we are moving toward an algorithmic environment. Technical analysis will be more like an engineering science. Technical analysis has been like a man without a horse—an observational science without the theory. Some people believe that the theory of nonlinear feedback exists and will be used to formally support technical analysis. We would leave the subjective art of the craft in the dust. The two- and four-week breakout rules should be easy to program. We could tell the computer to search for 15 percent jumps in one to three days to pick out the potential poles for flags and pennants. We could train a neural network system to search for patterns we haven't picked up from textbooks.

Third, we could see some sort of hybrid: the computer-generated patterns and the good old human brain side by side. The March 2009 issue of *Bloomberg Markets* magazine has a story on commodity trader Salem Abraham. During the 1987 stock market crash, he lost half of his futures account on bad currency trades. The lesson he learned was that you shouldn't trust what is taught in statistics class, because the things that one is taught can never happen, do, in fact, happen. In 2008 and into 2009, investors the world over have found that sophisticated formulas can go haywire and losses can happen despite massive back testing. These huge losses could spur algorithmic traders to look at charts, and chart watchers will learn to embrace computer-assisted pattern recognition. Investing shouldn't rely on just one approach to the exclusion of the others. No one approach is completely perfect and foolproof. We would all be better off if we had a philosophy of embracing all tools that add value. But even the best computer programmers should recognize that humans can recognize a new pattern faster than a computer.

Trying to profit from the reading and application of the chart and chart patterns may be difficult. There are problems in first recognizing the patterns on a timely basis or, better still, anticipating them somewhat. Patterns have variations with respect to shape (like complex head-and-shoulders patterns) and sometimes inconsistent volume characteristics, so that knowing all the patterns is the first point of difficulty. In Chapter 2, we noted that chart patterns are the result of human behavior, which can evolve over time and change to some extent. In addition, we as humans look at charts with our own biases. Since the early 1980s, the trading environment has changed and has become more volatile, in my opinion. Commodity markets probably were the first to become more volatile, but this has spilled over into the Standard & Poor's 500 Index futures, and ultimately, the broad equity market as money has become more concentrated in the hands of hedge fund managers. Money can and does move faster today by just a click of the mouse.

Can more math and computer programming be applied to chart patterns and chart reading? Perhaps, but considerable effort has already been expended on this effort, and we haven't heard of much success. Perhaps someone has been able to program some patterns successfully and they are very content to profit from their efforts and not share their results in a book or research article or through software sales. There are many creative analysts and many creative programmers, so we should expect that there are people who are trading on "patterns" in the data. The data may not be just price and volume, but may now include technical indicators and fundamental data. These new patterns could be used for looking at and analyzing intraday price action in addition to the daily price bars. I have spent many years looking at daily high, low, and close charts, but very little time looking at hourly or thirty-minute high, low, and close charts. It is possible that with enough hourly data and enough computer time that new patterns could appear that we were not able to detect. A starting point to find them might be to consult with and interview retired floor traders. Floor traders may have found some other repetitive price patterns that they used successfully. The famous Boy Plunger, Jessie Livermore, kept a record of price action on U.S. Steel in 1892 when he was just fifteen. We have no reason to believe that Livermore kept up charts, but he must have collected prices in a way that he could discern trends or patterns. Livermore supposedly made the observation that when a stock approached $100 per share, it would often trade up to $100. This probably would not be categorized as a classic chart pattern, but it is nevertheless a pattern in the price action Livermore found that persisted enough that he could profit from it. Perhaps someone's short-term observations of price swings will become a new pattern for other technically oriented traders of the future.

Assuming that there are some patterns in the intraday data that the computer can recognize and program, we may, in the future, have programs that search for patterns and flag them for traders. Along with the search, the computer could check how a pattern has worked before on one particular security and give the trader the probability of success in an up or down trend or a general bull or bear market. The program could also keep track of the variations that are possible, such as complex head-and-shoulders patterns, and could also put that in a report for the trader. Anything could be possible in the future. Even if we see more computers and programmers devoted to the market-place to ferret out patterns, the more that plain old human being is still needed. In January 2009, in a presentation at Bloomberg's New York offices, Professor Andrew Lo gave the following example.

One relative stumbled in the dining room during Thanksgiving dinner. The first time this relative stumbles, the thought was that it could be the alcohol being served. The second relative who stumbles is an aunt who doesn't drink. The human mind quickly comes to the conclusion that the carpet in the dinning room needs to be fixed, but the computer needs many more observations to reach that conclusion. The human mind is quicker than the computer in this instance. And it is likely to be that way with chart patterns.

Professor Lo and Jasmina Hasanhodzic have been working on making patterns more testable by defining technical patterns in terms of each pattern's geometric properties and constructing a kernel estimator of a series of prices so that its extremes can be given a "hard number." A *kernel regression estimator* means you don't know what form the solution will take, so you do what's called a *nonparametric fit* rather than a parametric fit. A parametric fit means that you know the answer is a straight line, for instance, but you don't know what the slope and location of the line are. A nonparametric fit means you have no idea if the answer looks like a straight line, a curve, or something funky. One of the best tools for nonparametric regression is the neural network.

Carol Osler and P. H. Kevin Chang wrote a paper in the October 1999 issue of *The Economic Journal* (Royal Economic Society, 1999, published by Blackwell Publishers) in which they looked at whether head-and-shoulders patterns are useful for predicting exchange-rate movements. Their study used daily exchange rates over some twenty years. "Methodical Madness: The Head-and-Shoulders Pattern in Foreign Exchange" found that head-and-shoulders patterns were pretty useful for forecasting exchange-rate movements, but that technical tools, such as moving averages or filter rules, were right more often. Perhaps the earliest venture at categorizing price patterns was conducted by Robert Levy in 1971. Levy used a five-point pattern system using a volatility filter. In the early 1980s, technical analyst Arthur A. Merrill applied the same five-point approach with an 8-percent filter. He put some order to the patterns by arranging them into two groups with the shape of the capital letters M and W.

Which of these three trends for the future will win out? Hard to say, but I see no downside in learning about the patterns that have endured for nearly a hundred years and adding them to your investment tool bag.

Index

About the Author

Bruce Kamich, CMT, is a vice president at Morgan Stanley Smith Barney's Technical Analysis Group and coauthors their flagship publication, the *Daily Technical Market Letter.* He also teaches technical analysis to various Morgan Stanley Smith Barney trading desks. Kamich has held a variety of positions related to research and technical analysis at firms such as McCarthy, Crisanti and Maffei; ALCO Commodities; and Merrill Lynch. He is an adjunct professor of finance at Baruch College and has also taught at Rutgers University, as well as being guest lecturer on many other campuses. He has twice served as president of the Market Technicians Association (MTA) and is currently president of the MTA Educational Foundation (MTAEF (www.mtaef.org)). Kamich is the author of *How Technical Analysis Works* (NYIF/Prentice Hall Press, 2002). He lives in New Jersey.

About Bloomberg

Bloomberg L.P., founded in 1981, is a global information services, news, and media company. Headquartered in New York, the company has sales and news operations worldwide.

Serving customers on six continents, Bloomberg, through its wholly-owned subsidiary Bloomberg Finance L.P., holds a unique position within the financial services industry by providing an unparalleled range of features in a single package known as the Bloomberg Professional® service. By addressing the demand for investment performance and efficiency through an exceptional combination of information, analytic, electronic trading, and straight-through-processing tools, Bloomberg has built a worldwide customer base of corporations, issuers, financial intermediaries, and institutional investors.

Bloomberg News, founded in 1990, provides stories and columns on business, general news, politics, and sports to leading newspapers and magazines throughout the world. Bloomberg Television, a 24-hour business and financial news network, is produced and distributed globally in seven languages. Bloomberg Radio is an international radio network anchored by flagship station Bloomberg 1130 (WBBR-AM) in New York.

In addition to the Bloomberg Press line of books, Bloomberg publishes *Bloomberg Markets* magazine.

To learn more about Bloomberg, call a sales representative at:

London: +44-20-7330-7500
New York: +1-212-318-2000
Tokyo: +81-3-3201-8900